CONTENTS

"Your scarf makes a
fine overcoat for me,
Mr. Editor!"

Published by the Victoria and Albert Museum 1983.
ISBN 0 905209 47 8
Copyright of illustrations: as listed.
Copyright of text: Kevin Carpenter.
Printed by Royle Print Limited.
Designed by Richard Sage.
Front Cover illustration Trevor Smith.

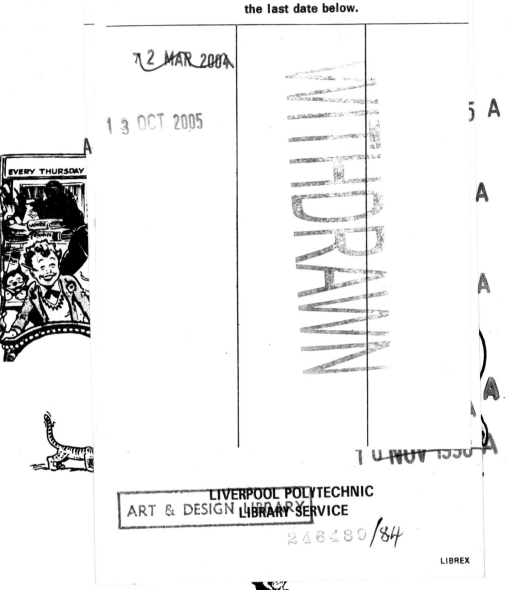

A loan exhibition from the
Library of Oldenburg University, West Germany
at the
Bethnal Green Museum of Childhood
2 June – 2 October 1983.

FOREWORD BY SIR ROY STRONG

Year by year the Bethnal Green Museum of Childhood is increasing the scope of its collections. For long it has been the V & A's Department of toys. In recent years it has been taking over and expanding the V & A's holdings of children's costume, children's furniture and other objects associated with childhood. Children's books also now come within its scope. Its own collection, in course of arrangement, must remain out of sight of the public for some years yet. But the Museum can signal its interest in the subject by exhibitions, such as the exhibition recorded in this catalogue, which is especially gratifying as it has brought the Museum into contact with another important collection of children's literature, that at the University of Oldenburg. We are most grateful to the University authorities and the University Librarian for lending the bulk of the exhibition; and special thanks are due to Kevin Carpenter, of the University's English Faculty, for devising the exhibition and writing the catalogue.

1

ACKNOWLEDGEMENTS

The compiler and publisher of this catalogue wish to thank the following for permission to reproduce copyright illustrations:

D.C.Thomson & Co.
Express Newspapers
IPC Magazines
Lutterworth Press
Routledge & Kegan Paul
Wells Gardner, Darton & Co.

They also thank D.C.Thomson & Co. and IPC Magazines for assistance in verifying matters of fact concerned with their publications; and emphasize that the compiler's opinions are his own and not necessarily those of D.C.Thomson & Co., IPC Magazines, or the Museum.

NOTE

This is a large exhibition with a total of some 350 items on display: story-papers, comics, posters, annuals, 'libraries', penny-part novels, original art-work and blow-ups. A precise description of every one of the exhibits would have meant producing a catalogue weighed down with a vast amount of detail, some of it repetitive. As this was neither practicable nor sensible, a different method of recording the main facts has been used. However many volumes or issues of any one periodical are on show, that periodical will have only one entry in the appropriate section, incorporating brief details of the full run of that publication. The only exceptions to this general rule are the penny-party novels in sections A, B and C, which are described in the catalogue as actually exhibited.

INTRODUCTION

Penny Dreadfuls and Comics is intended as a documentary history of children's periodical reading in England from the emergence of the first cheap boys' weeklies in the mid-Victorian age up to today's comics. The main criteria for the inclusion of papers in the exhibition were, simply, that they should have enjoyed considerable popularity in their time, and in content should have been primarily intended for amusement. These periodicals are interesting for a number of reasons. Some of them played a significant role in the development of children's literature in the nineteenth century, as they encouraged literary experimentation and consolidation. Seen as minor documents of social history, many of these papers offer a fascinating view of the past, reflecting the fads and fears of the age and recording the way life was seen by those involved. From an educational point of view, examining these children's periodicals may sharpen our awareness of the changing image of childhood, what was expected of boys as distinct from girls, the interests they were supposed to pursue, the attitude to life they were encouraged to adopt.

The main emphasis in the exhibition and catalogue however, is placed squarely on these papers as entertaining literature, for it was the kind of fiction they contained that made them at the same time popular and controversial.

The phrase 'penny dreadful'[1] encapsulates an attitude and an over-simplification. It was invented as a term of abuse to designate penny-part novels and cheap weekly periodicals, devoted mainly to tales of sensation and adventure and illustrated with lurid woodcuts, which were published for the amusement of working-class youth from the 1860's on. Just as the 'penny stinker' was a cheap and nasty cigar, so the 'penny dreadful' was considered a cheap and nasty boys' paper. There was general agreement amongst teachers, clergymen, magistrates and journalists that the penny dreadful glorified crime; that its boy-readers were tempted into a life of degradation and theft; that the amount of this garbage on the market was enormous; and that some kind of suppression should be placed on these publications. These were received truths, and few people actually bothered to examine the story-papers they assailed with such fury. Certainly, some of these booklets were shocking enough, brutal and inhuman, and deserved to be called 'dreadful.' But the expression 'penny dreadful' became a term of blanket condemnation, applied to the whole field of popular juvenile fiction which was scarcely justifiable.

Edward Salmon was one of the many contemporaries who attacked the 'degrading and debilitating dreadful', which he feared would inexorably lead to the 'moral and material ruin of the working class.'[2] Besides genuine anxiety about the spiritual well-being of the lower classes, a further reason for the uproar over cheap story-papers was hinted at in a lecture by Lord Shaftesbury in 1878:

[1] The earliest recorded use I have found of this term is in the 1874 edition of Hotten's **Slang Dictionary.**
[2] Edward Salmon, **Juvenile Literature As It Is,** London, 1888, chapter 8.

"It is creeping not only into the houses of the poor, neglected, and untaught, but into the largest mansions; penetrating into religious familes and astounding careful parents by its frightful issues."[3]

It would seem from this that the moral welfare of middle-class boys was at stake as well. It is perhaps worth noting that Lord Shaftesbury was addressing the Religious Tract Society, and that this body was so moved by its members' concern over the state of cheap juvenile fiction that it decided to bring out an antidote to the penny dreadful, publishing **The Boy's Own Paper** in 1879.

On one point, at least, the critics were right: the penny dreadfuls were enormously popular. Even before Forster's Education Act of 1870 introduced elementary education for all children, the literacy level amongst youngsters from working-class families was surprisingly high. Their appetite for escapist fiction, to judge from circulation figures, must have been voracious. Not many books were available to these children. Libraries catering for their interests did not emerge until late in the century. The price of children's books put out by the respectable publishing houses was prohibitive for ordinary families; **Alice in Wonderland** cost 6 shillings, something like a third of an industrial worker's average weekly wage. Many (working) youths could, however, afford a penny a week, or contributed their farthing towards 'clubs' which bought their favourite paper, or were given a ragged, read-to-death copy of the previous week's issue. Contemporary observers estimated that on average each copy of these periodicals was shared by around nine readers. This would mean that the **Boys of England,** the most important of these cheap papers, with its peak circulation of 250,000 copies was actually read by more than two million children per week. (The titles may suggest that the penny dreadful was geared to boys' reading interests, but there is evidence to show that girls were equally avid readers.)

There is a clear line of descent from the penny dreadfuls, through the tuppeny bloods of the inter-war period, to modern adventure comics for boys. The continuity is descernable in theme, static characterization, concentration on incident, and illustrative style. Even the speech balloon, it could be argued, continues the emphasis the dreadful laid on dialogue. There are, however, as this exhibition shows, both story-papers and comics which do not belong to that tradition.

Although sales have been falling since the post-war peak, there are still more comics published per child in this country than in any other European country.[4] The 1950s saw the most rapid expansion of the comics market; in the same decade most of the old story-papers became extinct. As the visual image became dominant, the

---

[3]Cit. Patrick Dunae, 'Penny Dreadfuls: Late Nineteenth-Century Boys' Literature and Crime', in **Victorian Studies,** vol. 22, 1979.

[4]The following figures on British comics sales have been put together from various sources: 16 million copies per week in the 1950s; 8 million in the 1960s; 10½ million in the 1970s; less than 7 million copies per week in the early 1980s. Additionally, approaching 3 million copies of boys' and girls' magazines are sold each week.

text shrank to a few hundred words a page. TV is often blamed for this dominance of the image, but it was not only television as a medium which accelerated this change. After his or her daily two-and-a-half hour dose of the box, today's child has little time for light reading. Publishers of children's papers had to come up with something that could be consumed in a fraction of the time spent on the old 40,000-word bloods; the answer was stories in picture-form with a minimum of accompanying words in captions and speech balloons.

The decrease in the number of words in the popular comics (**Beano** actually began as a mixture of comic strips and conventional serialised story) has been widely deplored as a factor in falling reading standards in Britain, and this is not the only criticism levelled against the comics. They restrict children's fantasy, it is said, present people as stereotypes, appeal to the immature mind, and propagate an immoral picture of the world. Some of these arguments will be familiar to those who have studied Victorian popular literature and the way public opinion responded to it, and this 'bad press' is one of the continuities involved here.

Comics have, however, had their advocates. It has been argued on the one hand that they are simply old-fashioned, harmless fun; on the other that they provide an imaginative arena where children can work out their own inner conflicts. Surprisingly enough, so far as I know, no-one has attempted to examine the specific picture-plus-word character of the comic. The decrease in words has been noted, but what about the concomitant increase in pictures and what about the way a child decodes these combinations?

All in all, little has been written to date about the development of children's magazines and comics in Britain. There are only dotted references in the standard history of English children's books,[5] and for all Denis Gifford's tireless efforts, the history of English comics is still waiting to be written. The only general study of the whole field is E. S. Turner's **Boys Will Be Boys,** a very sound and entertaining guide which was first published as long ago as 1948 (a revised edition was recently issued in Penguin). One reason for the dearth of studies of popular juvenile fiction is the scarcity of primary material. Most of these penny dreadfuls and comics were read to bits or thrown away by their young readers. Some children (or parents) may have taken G. A. Henty's advice to heart: 'Put the pernicious things into the fire!'[6]

The title of this exhibition may be catchy, but it is something of a misnomer, as some of the papers on display can be categorized neither as penny dreadfuls nor as comics. In fact, one of the largest sections is devoted to periodicals put out by the respectable publishers, magazines such as **The Boy's Own Paper, Chums** and **Aunt Judy's Magazine,** which parents in well-off families readily accepted and subscribed to for their children. To do justice to the full scope of the juvenile

[5]F. J. Harvey Darton, **Children's Books in England** (revised by Brian Alderson), Cambridge, 1982.
[6]**Beeton's Boy's Own Magazine**, vol. 1, no. 9, September 1889.

periodical in England, and for the sake of comparison with the pulp put out for the entertainment of children from working-class families, a considerable amount of this material has been included. It is in this section (E) that the work of some of the best-known children's writers (Juliana Ewing, G. A. Henty, John Buchan, Jules Verne and others) and illustrators (Gordon Browne, George Cruikshank, Ernest Griset, Wal Paget and many more) is on display.

The bulk of the historical material on show has been selected from collections of 'respectable' children's periodicals, rare comics (covering the period 1890 to 1939), and penny dreadfuls, belonging to the Library of the University of Oldenburg in West Germany. (Further items have been kindly lent by private collectors.) It is, perhaps unconventional for an academic institution to purchase this kind of material, but the University of Oldenburg has a special interest in children's literature. In co-operation with the City of Oldenburg and the College of Adult Education, the University (founded in 1974) has organised an annual non-commercial children's book fair since 1975, and has mounted four exhibitions of historical children's books largely based on the Library's own holdings. A fifth exhibition, on girls' books in Europe, is in preparation.

Penny Dreadfuls and Comics is a large exhibition and is more than one person could have coped with alone. I have been fortunate in having a lot of generous help while I was putting it together for the University of Oldenburg in 1981 and re-organising it for the London showing. My thanks are due to Derek Adley, Brian Alderson, Leo Baxendale, Avril Carpenter, Pia Carpenter, Jens-Ulrich Davids, Denis Gifford, Deidre Graydon, Ron Holland, Louis James, Bill Lofts, Manfred Schramme, Norman Shaw, Richard Stinshoff, the librarians at Oldenburg University Library and the British Library, and Anthony Burton, Peter Glenn and Halina Pasierbska at the Bethnal Green Museum of Childhood.

Kevin Carpenter

EDWIN J. BRETT'S
'WILD AND WONDERFUL FICTION'

Cheap fiction for Victorian youth was dominated by the figure of Edwin John Brett.[1] The son of an officer and a minor participant in the Chartist movement, Brett first became involved in publishing as a writer and engraver, then as the manager of the ill-famed Newsagents' Publishing Company. He was responsible in the mid-1860s for the publication of the kind of 'gallow's literature' which outraged public opinion: stories about pirates, highwaymen, and sordid crime in the metropolis, bearing such titles as **Black Rollo, the Pirate** (1864-65), **Red Ralph** (1865-66), **The Dance of Death** (1865-66) and the notorious **Wild Boys** series.[2] These were novels, sold in penny weekly parts, each part consisting of eight pages of text embellished with a lurid illustration. It is hardly surprising that these booklets, which presented scenes of crime, murder and debauchery in loving detail, were branded 'penny dreadfuls.'

Brett, shrewd businessman that he was, soon realized that he would not be able to exploit the rapidly expanding market by ignoring public opinion and catering to the lowest tastes of his readers, and did a quick about-turn, cleaning up his own publications overnight and launching his own attack on others still publishing 'vile penny books.' He determined to preserve an air of respectability in his own boys' papers, without, however alienating his adolescent readers with their insatiable appetite for adventure and sensation. The result was what he called 'wild and wonderful fiction,' quietly adding, with a nod towards his young readers' parents, that it was at the same time 'honest and pure.'

Brett's **annus mirabilis** was 1866. He had already experimented with two short-lived, small-format magazines, **The Boy's Companion** (1865), and **The Boy's Own Reader** (1866), exploring the idea of a boy's miscellany, the backbone of which would be fiction, but including other material as well: articles on hobbies and sport, letters, poems, anecdotes, competitions. He was evidently impressed by two highly successful weeklies for working-class adult readers, the **London Journal** and **Reynolds's Miscellany,** for he quite openly imitated their format, layout, illustrative style and melodramatic content in his new venture, simply adding an elaborate masthead and calling the end-product **The Boys of England.** It was first issued on 24 November 1866 and appeared every week until 30 June 1899.

The main aim of **The Boys of England,** according to 'The Editor's Address' (reprinted in this catalogue), was to 'enthral' its young readers with thrilling fiction, and the editor felt satisfied to imagine boys returning home from school, office, shop and factory and taking up a copy of the story-paper to 'soothe and enliven [their] "care-tired thoughts." This fiction was provided by such writers as Captain Mayne

---

[1] On Brett and his publications, see Louis James, 'Tom Brown's Imperialist Sons,' in **Victorian Studies,** vol. 17, September 1973.

[2] When one of this series was reprinted by G. Farrah in 1877 it was suppressed by the police (according to **The Times** of 13 December 1877).

A

Reid, Percy and Vane St. John, W. H. Stephens, Cecil Stagg and others[3] The first editorial went on to say that it was created for boys who intended to make something out of their lives. For such boys, **The Boys of England** contained advice about various occupations open to working-class youth, and snippets from Samuel Smiles's **Self-Help.** Another significant element of the new paper was its patriotic tone, sounded in the first of a series of articles on the history of Britain, intended to display the strengths of English national character, particularly 'that true manliness, which is the cause of England's moral as well as physical supremacy over the other nations of the earth'.

Three quarters of the space in **The Boys of England** was, however, devoted to serialized fiction, the opening serial being **Alone in the Pirates' Lair** by Charles Stevens. Both author and publisher went to great pains to emphasize that pirates were not being glamorized in this story, but were presented for what they really were, loathsome villains. The hero of the piece is a young, bold midshipman, Jack Rushton, who pits his wits and daring against the pirates, slaughtering the whole gang virtually single-handed. After the final triumph of Good over Evil, during the course of which much blood is spilt, the fifteenth and final instalment concludes with these cautionary words:

> "Now if there be any of our boy readers who have felt an inclination to sympathise with or admire "dashing rovers" and "bold buccaneers," let him reflect on the dark deeds of the false, cruel, and bloodthirsty Don Pablo, and recall the perils and sufferings of our hero, Jack Rushton, during the eventful time which he spent "Alone in the Pirates' Lair."

The Boys of England was an immediate success, initially selling around 150,000 copies per week, four times more than Brett's earlier penny-part novels. Its companion paper **Young Men of Great Britain** (1868) reached similar sales. In 1867 Brett became sole proprietor of the Newsagents' Publishing Company, changing the name in 1870 to The "Boys of England" Office. The circulation of **The Boys of England** soared to 250,000 copies in 1871 when it began to serialize stories written by Bracebridge Hemyng about an ebullient young man he called Jack Harkaway.[4] In the same year Brett began to remove the most popular serials from his two boys' papers and sell them separately in penny weekly parts, then shilling volumes with chromographed wrappers.

---

[3]For brief biographies of these and many other boys' writers, see W. O. G. Lofts and D. J. Adley, **The Men Behind Boys' Fiction,** London, 1970.

[4]Brett's Harkaway series appeared in his **Boys of England,** 1871-76; **Our Boys' Journal,** 1878-79; **Jack Harkaway's Journal for Boys,** 1879; **Up-to-Date Boys,** 1899-1900; **Boys of the Empire,** 1904-5. The American series was reprinted in Britain in **The Young Briton** and **The Young Englishman,** 1874-78. George Newnes also published a Harkaway story in his **British Boys** in 1896. The name Harkaway was possibly borrowed from a race-horse in **Tom Brown's Schooldays,** 1857, or from a story which appeared in **The Young Briton** in 1870 under the title **Hark-Away Jack.**

Of Brett's subsequent publications, **Our Boys' Journal** (1876) was moderately successful, but Brett's only incursion into the girls' sector of the market, **Our Girls' Journal** (1882) was a flop, only surviving for two months. **The Boys' Sunday Reader** (1879) was Brett's abortive attempt to pre-empt the boys' paper known to be in preparation under the auspices of the Religious Tract Society. **The Boys' Comic Journal** (1883) was concocted according to the by now traditional recipe, its main ingredient being the adventure serial in mock historical setting. **Boys of the Empire** (1888) was a reprint paper, but is worthy of note as the first juvenile periodical in Britain regularly printed throughout in full colour. At 1½d it was fifty per cent more expensive than other story-papers, and youngsters apparently preferred to keep the halfpenny and make do with black and white; after a year the attractive colour printing disappeared and the price reverted to a penny. Shortly before his death, Brett brought out the small-format magazine **The Halfpenny Surprise** (1894) as his response to the challenge issued by Alfred Harmsworth with his cheap papers and comics. These are probably the most important of the twenty-eight boys' periodicals issued by Brett and his successors up to the close of the nineteenth century.

Advert for the penny-part novel **May Turpin,** 1864.

The first issue of **Boys of England** is dated Saturday,
24 November 1866 (with some copies dated 27 November).
Charles Stevens penned the opening serial **Alone in the
Pirates' Lair,** which was illustrated by Esmond
Hebblethwaite.

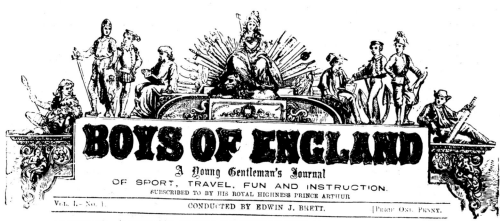

"HIS FINGERS TOUCH THE PISTOL—THE PIRATE EMITS A DEEP, FIERCE GROWL."

ALONE IN THE PIRATES' LAIR
BY THE EDITOR.

CHAPTER I.
HOMEWARD BOUND.

THE good ship 'Titania', homeward bound from Canton, and laden with a costly cargo, lies at anchor off the Ladrones.

Leaning lightly against the taffrail, a young midshipman gazed dreamingly, through the glowing, limitless expanse of blending sky and sea.

"Aha! here it comes at last!"

The boy started, and looked round inquiringly.

The first-mate, who had stepped to his side unobserved by him, uttered this exclamation in a tone of intense satisfaction.

"Aye, sir; in yonder cloud to starboard?"

"Yes, Mr. Rushton, that little cloud, not bigger than a man's hand, and soon we shall have it in right earnest; be so good as to call the captain."

"Aye, sir," returned the mid, touching his cap, respectfully.

He stepped nimbly from the quarter-deck, went below, and tapped at the captain's door.

"Come in."

The boy entered.

"Wind, Mr. Rushton?"

"Aye, sir."

"Which way?"

"North-west and by north, sir."

"Good! tell Mr. Dale to heave anchor at once; I'll be on deck in a few moments."

"Aye, sir."

Soon the boatswain's whistle rung shrilly along the quiet deck.

The crew came tumbling up the hatchways, or sprung from the forecastle and from under the bulwarks.

"All hands up anchor, ahoy!" was the boatswain's gruff shout.

The fifer struck up a jaunty air.

"Man the bars!"

And then came the order, "Heave around!"

Forty sturdy tars tramp, tramp, tramped around, their broad, brawny shoulders bearing hard against the capstan-bars, and their bare, light-tripping

The Boy's Comic Journal, Stories of Fun, Adventure and Romance. London: Edwin J. Brett. Ed. by E. J. Brett. 788 nos. in 31 vols. 17 March 1883 to 16 April 1898.
Beginning with no. 589 dated 23 June 1894 each issue has an 8-page Novelette. This story-paper was discontinued after a fire at the printers, Vincent Brooks, Day & Son.

Boys of the Empire (Boys of the Empire and Young Men of Great Britain, 1889-93). London: Edwin J. Brett. Ed. by E. J. Brett. 277 nos. in 11 vols. 6 February 1888 to 22 May 1893.
Printed in colour up to no. 51, 21 January 1889, then mauve ink to no. 72, 17 June 1889, thereafter black.

Boys of the Empire (Boys of the Empire, An Up-to-Date Boys' Journal, 1901-6). London: Edwin J. Brett Ltd./ Harkaway House. 311 nos. in 29 quarterly volumes (divisions). 9 October 1900 to 22 September 1906.

Boys of England (Boys of England and Jack Harkaway's Journal of Travel, Fun and Instruction, 1893-96). London: Newsagents' Publishing Company/ Edwin J. Brett. Ed. by Charles Stevens (first 9 issues)/ E. J. Brett. 1,702 weekly nos. in 66 vols. 24/27 November 1866 to 30 June 1899.
Initial circulation 150,000 copies p.w. rising to 250,000 in the 1870s. From no. 1,440 dated 22 June 1894 each number contains an 8-page Novelette.

Boys of England Re-issue. 574 issues in 22 vols. 20 April 1874 to 14 April 1885.
Short-lived revival **New Boys of England** ran for only 14 weeks from 22 September to 22 December 1906.

The Boy's Own Reader, A Magazine of Instruction and Recreation for the Young. London: Newsagents' Publishing Company. Ed. by Rev. G. D'Arcy Irvine M.A. 23 nos. 1 January to 5 June 1866.

The Boys'-Sunday-Reader, A Magazine of Pure Literature. London: Edwin J. Brett. Ed. by E. J. Brett. 52 nos. in 2 vols. 8 January to 31 December 1879. Continued as **The Boys'-Weekly-Reader.** 1880 (52 nos.?)

Boys'-Weekly-Reader Novelette. London: Edwin J. Brett. Ed. by E. J. Brett. Commenced 4 March 1881 and seems to have been discontinued in 1886.

The Halfpenny Surprise. London: Edwin J. Brett. 600 issues. 2 November 1894 to 28 April 1906.

Our Boy's Journal, A Weekly Magazine for Every Home. London: Edwin J. Brett. Ed. by E. J. Brett. 330 nos. in 12 vols. 30 August 1876 to 27 December 1882.

Up-to-Date Boys, Journal & Novelettes. London: Edwin J. Brett Ltd. 104 issues in 8 quarterly vols. (divisions). 30 June 1899 to 21 June 1901.

Young Men of Great Britain, A Journal of Amusing and Instructive Literature. Companion to the **Boys of England.** London: Newsagents' Publishing Company/Edwin J. Brett. Ed. by Vane St. John. 1,117 issues in 44 vols. 29 January 1868 to 17 June 1889.
Initial circulation 150,000 copies p.w.

Young Men of Great Britain Re-issue. 430 nos., 4 November 1874 to 30 January 1883.

The cloth-bound, half-yearly volumes of Brett's boys papers, at 4 shillings a piece, were evidently produced for boys from well-to-do families.

Penny-part novels.

The Black Cavalier; or, The Banner of England. London: "Boys of England" Office, [ca. 1890]. 13 parts. pp. 198.
Written by Robert Justyn Lambe and originally serialized in **Boys of England** from 20 January to 15 June 1888.

Black Rollo, the Pirate; or, The Dark Woman of the Deep: A Graphic Tale of the American War. Founded on Facts. London: Newsagents' Publishing Company, [1864-65]. 93 parts. pp. 742.
By Captain Irving Lyons.

The Boyhood Days of Guy Fawkes; or, The Conspirators of Old London. London: "Boys of England" Office, [ca. 1885]. 12 parts. pp. 184.
By R. J. Lambe and originally appeared as a serial in **Young Men of Great Britain** from 12 March to 25 June 1885.

The Boy Sailor; or, Life on Board a Man-of-War. London: Newsagents' Publishing Co., 1865. 33 parts. pp. 260.
By Captain Lyons. Reprinted under the title **Harry Halliard** in Brett's **Boys' Library** in 1879.

By Command of the King; or, The Days of the Merrie Monarch. London: Harkaway House, [ca. 1890]. 12 parts. pp. 188.
Lambe's first historical novel for E. J. Brett was serialized in **Boys of England** from 12 January to 20 April 1883.

The Dance of Death; or, The Hangman's Plot. A thrilling Romance of Two Cities. London: Newsagents' Publishing Co., [11 November 1865] to 7 April 1866. 23 parts. pp. 182.

Edwin J. Brett's Adventures of Young Jack Harkaway and his Boy Tinker. London: "Boys of England" Office, [1877?] 14 parts. pp. 222.
Serial in the **Boys of England** from 7 January to 10 November 1876. E. J. Brett is the publisher, not the author.

Jack Harkaway's Schooldays. London: 173 Fleet Street [i.e. Edwin John Brett], 1873. 17 parts. pp. 188.
Written by Bracebridge Hemyng, the first in the popular Harkaway series was serialized in vols. 10 and 11 of **Boys of England** from 19 August 1871 to 6 January 1872.

Jack-o'-the-Cudgel; or, The Hero of a Hundred Fights. London: E. J. Brett, [ca. 1890]. 11 parts. pp. 172.
Serialized in **Boys of England** from 5 June to 24 December 1875 and issued in penny-parts in February 1876. The author is William M'Gonogall.

May Turpin, the Queen of the Road. A Romance. London: Newsagents' Publishing Company. 1864.
This novel seems to have been discontinued after only a few weeks, if it appeared at all. Above title from an advert.

Red Ralph; or, The Daughter of the Night. A Romance of the Road in the Days of Dick Turpin. London: Published for the London Romance Company by the Newsagents' Publishing Company, [1865-66?]. 52 parts. pp. 412.
Written by Percival Wolfe and illustrated by Robert Prowse.

The Sword of Fate; or, The Headsman's Doom. London: "Boys of England" Office, [ca. 1890]. 14 parts. pp. 220.
By R. J. Lambe and first published in **Boys of the Empire** from 6 August 1888 to 18 March 1889.

Tom Floremall's Schooldays. London: Harkaway House, [ca. 1895]. 16 parts. pp. 264.
Serialized in **Boys of England** from 11 February to 6 October 1876 and issued in penny-parts the following year.

The Young Apprentice; or, The Watchwords of Old London. London: Harkaway House, [ca. 1895]. 33 parts in 2 vols. pp. 516.
By Vane Ireton St. John and originally issued in 65 penny-parts in 1867-68. Some of the illustrations are engraved by E. J. Brett.

Poster advertising one of the stories in the Jack Harkaway saga.

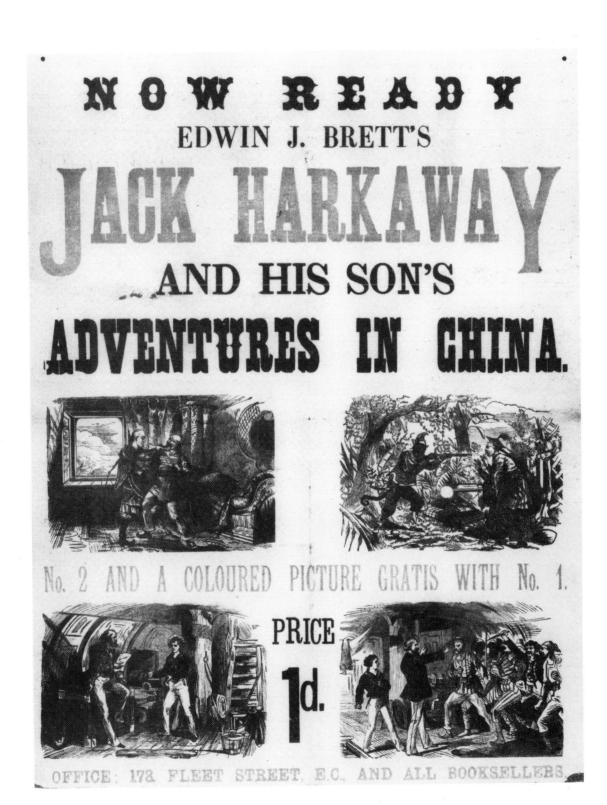

E. J. Brett's **Boys of the Empire** was printed in full colour
by the Leighton Brothers. This issue is dated 2 July 1888.

18

The peculiar blend of facetiousness, suspense, violence,
and hero-worship which made up the penny dreadful is well
captured on this cover for the last story in Brett's Harkaway
series.

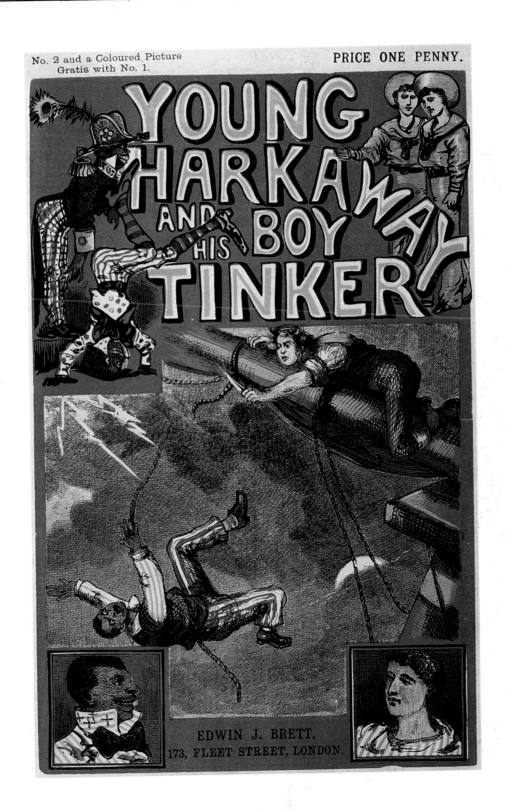

BRETT'S COMPETITORS AND THEIR 'PENNY PACKETS OF POISON'

E. J. Brett and his arch-rivals, the Emmett brothers,[1] used to hurl insults at each other across Fleet Street, and the mutual denigration spilt over into the editorials and correspondence columns of their boys' periodicals as well. The Emmetts accused Brett of hypocrisy and cut-throat exploitation of his staff; Brett charged the 'unprincipled and uneducated' Emmetts with cashing in on his ideas.[2] In the late sixties, the two firms brought out around a dozen boys' papers which, superficially at least, looked alike and had strikingly similar titles. As their reply to Brett's **Boys of England** (1866), the Emmetts issued **The Young Englishman** (1867); Brett's **Young Men of Great Britain** (1868) was capped by their **Young Gentlemen of Britain** (1868), and so on. This jealous rivalry reached its ludicrous height on 11 March 1872 when both publishers brought out periodicals with unusual, but suspiciously similar, titles; Brett had **Rovers of the Sea,** and the Emmetts, **The Rover's Log.**

In the long run, however, Brett had the last laugh. His periodicals appealed to teenagers in all social classes, where those issued by his rivals were mainly purchased by boys from the lowest social stratum: sons of unskilled workers, errand boys, grocery assistants, young lads from the East End slums. Such boys would scarcely have been able to afford a subscription, but would have bought copies sporadically, whenever they could afford it. The fluctuating and unpredictable circulation of the Emmetts' papers was doubtless one reason why their firm, Hogarth House, went bankrupt around 1875 and was taken over by their former manager, Charles Fox. Another cause of their lack of success resided in the poor quality of the pulp they issued, stories about a wide range of crooks, murderers, pirates, highwaymen, and beings with supernatural powers. While Brett had carefully toned down the horrific element in his story-papers, the Emmetts' material put out in the sixties and early seventies tended to be gory and emphatically sensational.

One of the writers working for the Hogarth House periodicals – **The Young Briton, Sons of Britannia** and **The Young Englishman** – was the prolific Edwin Harcourt Burrage, who began his career writing facetious school stories containing strong elements of slapstick. He took over **Tom Wildrake's Schooldays,** (1870-73), when the original author, George Emmett, found himself out of his depth. Burrage turned a mediocre yarn into a bestseller, and a novel which established a formula for later boys' writers to follow. After riotous years at a public school, young heroes were then sent to the colonies to fight for the flag (Tom is shipped to India, then Australia). This became the standard career for a many a young hero, provided, of course, he found favour with his readers. Burrage later branched out into adventure

---

[1]George, Henry Charlton, William Laurence, and Robert. A sister, Sophie, was at one point also involved in the family's publishing affairs.

[2]For an account of this feud, see Ralph Rollington, **A Brief History of Boys' Journals,** Leicester, 1913.

B

of a more sensational flavour. In his **Handsome Harry** (1876), a story based on the revenge theme, he created a whole gallery of vivid characters, among them one Ching-Ching, a wiry, crafty, amiable Chinese sailor who always popped up in the nick of time to rescue his master from some fix or other. Burrage wrote the Ching-Ching series for Charles Fox's **Boys' Standard** and **Boys' Leisure Hour** between 1876 and 1886, continuing the saga in his own boys' paper **Ching-Ching's Own** (1888-93). For Fox, Burrage also penned **Broad-Arrow Jack,** another revenge story, and a novel with a powerful undercurrent of sadism and cruelty; it was in fact one of the books instanced in the press as being completely unsuitable for impressionable youth.

All the publishers included in this section came in for considerable stick at the hands of journalists, who derided their periodicals as 'penny packets of poison'.[3] The list of these publishers begins with the Emmetts. Operating from behind names ranging from John Milbank Crisp to Temple Publishing Company, they issued a variety of boys' papers and highwayman and pirate tales. Then there was Charles Fox, who brought out such shockers as **Sweeney Todd, Three-Fingered Jack,** and **Spring-Heeled Jack.** Samuel Dacre Clarke owned the Popular Publishing Company, writing and editing virtually all his own material under the *nom-de-plume* Guy Rayner. While Ralph Rollington (or rather J. W. Allingham) was publishing **The Boy's World** and **Our Boys' Paper,** Charles Perry Brown, proprietor of the Aldine Publishing Company, was busy organising the import of dime novels from the States (see section D). Edward Harrison of Salisbury Square was a notorious figure in the trade, well-known for his highwayman series (see section C). Towards the end of the century Charles Shurey tried his luck with **Comrades,** only to find the nineties a bad time for beginners without solid financial backing. Two publishers of cheap fiction for teenagers were spared outright condemnation in the press. E. J. Brett was sometimes included, although his papers were generally regarded as mindless but inoffensive. Indeed, one of the crusaders against trashy literature, James Greenwood, actually joined Brett's staff as a story-writer in 1868. The other exception was James Henderson, publisher of **Young Folks,** which serialized R. L. Stevenson's **Treasure Island** in the winter of 1881-82; Henderson was generally let off lightly, although his plots were castigated as extravagant. If any one of the above publishers was singled out for censure, it was Charles Fox. In 1890 an incensed **Quarterly Review** investigator has this to say of his books:

"In a lane not far from Fleet Street [i.e. Shoe Lane] there is a complete factory of the literature of rascaldom – a literature which has done much to people our prisons, our reformatories, and our Colonies, with scapegraces and ne'er-do-wells'.[4]

[3] The phrase is from James Greenwood's article 'A Short Way to Newgate', reprinted in his **The Wilds of London,** London, 1874.

[4] [Francis Hitchman], 'Penny Fiction', in **The Quarterly Review,** vol. 171, July 1890.

Story-papers and 'libraries'.
('Libraries' in this sense are small-format magazines
published on an irregular basis.)

The Boys' Graphic. London: Popular Publishing Company.
Ed. by Guy Rayner [i.e. Samuel Dacre Clarke]. 52 nos. in
2 vols. 8 March 1890 to 28 February 1891.

Boy's Herald, Entertaining, Instructive and Useful.
London: John Dicks. 100 nos. in 4 vols. 6 January 1877 to
30 November 1878.

The Boys' Illustrated News, The First Illustrated
Newspaper for the Young. London: Thomas Fox. Ed. by
Captain Mayne Reid and John Latey Jnr. 61 issues.
6 April 1881 to 8 June 1882.

The Boy's Leisure Hour, A Re-issue of the Favourite
Journal **The Boy's Standard.** London: Charles Fox.
379 nos. 23 August 1884 to 21 November 1891.

The Boy's Standard. London: Charles Fox.
1st series: 288 nos; 6 November 1875 to 7 May 1881.
2nd series: 580 nos; 14 May 1881 to 18 June 1892.

The Boy's World. London: James W. Allingham. 404 nos.
12 April 1879 to 27 December 1886.

British Boys, The Best and Biggest Halfpenny Boys'
Paper in the World. London: George Newnes. 104 weekly
nos. 12 December 1896 to 3 December 1898.

Ching-Ching Yarns. London: T. Harrison Roberts. 8 issues.
[ca. 1895].

Complete Sensational Library. London:
17 Gough Square, Fleet Street. At least 10 nos. [ca. 1895].

Comrades, Largest Published Boys' Book. London:
Charles Shurey. Ed. by Charles Shurey. 148 nos. in 3 vols.
14 January 1893 to 1 October 1895.
Reprint: 63 nos. in 4 divisions, 17 January 1898 to
6 March 1899.

The Gentleman's Journal and Youth's Miscellany of
Literature, Information & Amusement. London: E. Harrison
& E. Viles. 150 issues in 6 vols. 1 November 1869 to
12 September 1872.
The monthly parts have a 24-page Recreation Supplement.
Companion paper to **The Young Ladies' Journal**
(see below).

Our Boys' Paper. London: 12, 13 and 14 Fetter Lane
[i.e. James W. Allingham]. 117 nos. in 3 vols.
18 November 1880 to 31 January 1883.

The Young Briton, A Journal of Fact and Fiction, Sport and
Science/Journal of Romance and Amusing Literature.
London: George Brent & William Emmet Laurence/
Henry Lea/Charles Fox, Hogarth House, for the proprietor
[i.e. George Emmett]. Ed. by George Emmett. 433 nos.
18 September 1869 to 20 October 1877.
The numbering of volume and issue is erratic.

The Young Englishman. London: Charles Fox,
Hogarth House, for the proprietor [i.e. George Emmett].
Ed. by George Emmett. 336 issues in 13 vols. 19 April 1873
to 6 September 1879.

The Young Ladies' Journal. London: E. Harrison &
Walter Viles.
2,906 issues in 95 vols. 13 April 1864 to 5 June 1920.
Companion paper to **The Gentleman's Journal**
(see above).

A lurid illustration by Harry Maguire for an equally
gruesome tale by J. J. G. Bradley in **The Young
Englishman** dated 10 May 1873.

Penny-part novels.

Broad-Arrow Jack. London: Hogarth House, [ca. 1890].
24 parts. pp. 243.
Written by E. H. Burrage and illustrated by Harry Maguire.
Appeared as a serial in Fox's Boy's Standard in 1878.

Caractacus, the Champion of the Arena. London:
Hogarth House, [ca. 1880]. 11 parts. pp. 110.
Written by Charles Stevens, illustrated by Hary Maguire,
and serialized in **The Boys' Standard** in 1876.

For Valour; or, How I Won The Victoria Cross. London:
Hogarth House, [ca. 1880]. 13 parts. pp. 142.
By George Emmett, with illustrations by Harry Maguire.
A story in the series **Shot and Shell** and originally
serialized in **The Young Briton** from 30 October 1869 to
23 April 1870. Penny-part issue from May to July 1871.

Handsome Harry of the Fighting 'Belvedere.' London:
Hogarth House, [ca. 1880]. 28 parts. pp. 279.
Edwin Harcourt Burrage is the author, Hary Maguire the
illustrator. Appeared as a serial in **The Boys' Standard**
in 1876.

The King's Hussars. A Tale of India. London:
Hogarth House, [ca. 1880]. 16 parts. pp. 250.
A military story by George Emmett from the series

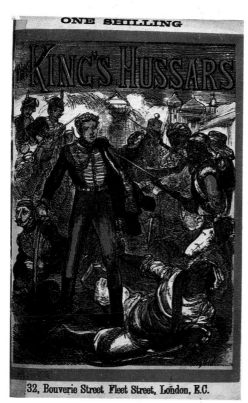

One of the many boys' stories about the Indian Mutiny
of 1857.

Shot and Shell, with illustrations by Harry Maguire. First
appearance in **The Young Englishman's Journal** in 1869.
On the Queen's Service. A Tale of Many Lands. London:
Hogarth House, [ca. 1880]. 12 parts. pp. 120.
J. J. G. Bradley's novel, illustrated by Warwick Reynolds Snr.,
appeared in **The Boys' Standard** in 1875-76 and came out
in weekly parts in early 1879; it was reprinted in **The Boys'
Leisure Hour** in 1884-85 and 1889-90.

Out on the World. London: Hogarth House, [ca. 1875].
8 parts. pp. 88.
A shorter version of this circus story by George Emmett,
illustrated by Harry Maguire, had appeared in **The Young
Englishman's Journal** from 13 April to 3 May 1867.
Shaw, the Lifeguardsman. London: Hogarth House,
[ca. 1880]. 21 parts. pp. 292.
Another tale from the series **Shot and Shell** by
George Emmett and originally a serial in **The Young
Englishman's Journal** in 1868-69, then penny-parts in
1872. Illustrations by Hary Maguire.

Tom Wildrake's Schooldays. London: Hogarth House,
[ca. 1875]. 63 parts. pp. 890.
Credited on the title-page to George Emmett, but actually
written by E. H. Burrage. Illustrated by Hary Maguire.
Appeared as a serial in **Sons of Britannia,** 1870-73.

Young Tom's Schooldays. London: Hogarth House,
[ca. 1880]. 18 parts. pp. 212.
Although George Emmett appears on the title-page as the
author, this school yarn was probably penned by
E. H. Burrage. It was originally printed in **The Young
Englishman** from 26 July 1873 to 14 March 1874 with
illustrations by Hary Maguire and 'Phiz'
[i.e. Hablot K. Browne].

'Phiz' (Hablot K. Browne) illustrated many of the humorous
stories published by the Emmett brothers and Charles Fox.
The above illustration is from the serial **Benjamin
Badluck's Schooldays,** 1874.

A typical Hogarth House wrapper.

ONE SHILLING & SIXPENCE.

YOUNG TOM'S SCHOOLDAYS

LONDON:—HOGARTH HOUSE, BOUVERIE STREET, FLEET STREET E.C.

OUTLAWS AND CRIMINALS AS HEROES

The most popular Victorian penny dreadful was a highwayman novel. Edward Viles' **Black Bess,** so named after Dick Turpin's favourite mare, was published in penny weekly parts for a full five years, from the spring of 1863 to the spring of 1868.[1] Frequently re-issued up to the 1890s, by which time the stereotype plates were so cracked and worn down that dozens of pages were replaced by brief synopses, its total sales were rumoured at around two million copies. Viles folowed up his success by writing two sequels, **The Black Highwayman** and **Blueskin.**

In the second weekly part of **Black Bess** the author defended the highwayman story against the criticism that the thoughtless were tempted into imitating the crimes portrayed there (his own Dick Turpin had just robbed the Lord Mayor of London), by pointing out rather sarcastically that in the age of the train there were no stagecoaches left to hold up. The highwayman story was a romance about a past era, he went on, wild and wonderful adventure eagerly read by people whose lives were monotonous and void of excitement. And was it not true that historical reality was softened in many romances of chivalry; yet no-one would think of stigmatizing the mailed knight or crusader.

"In fact, the bold highwayman who cried "Stand and deliver!" upon the road, has got to be considered in the light of a species of knight-errant, whose chief business was to redress such social wrongs as came under his immediate notice in the course of the many adventures among high and low, which must necessarily fall to his lot, and this is why we follow him with pleasure. Were scenes of violence alone depicted, the only feeling that would be called into existence would be disgust at his atrocities. Such, then, being the case, it must be self-evident that it is not his obnoxiousness to the laws of the land nor the crimes of which he may have been guilty, that rivets the attention of the reader, but his courage, address, single-mindedness, and opposition to all kinds of oppression."

All that is needed to round off this idealized picture of the highwayman is some hint of his having been maliciously 'framed' by his half-brother and deprived of his rightful inheritance, and the desperate footpad becomes a Robin Hood figure.

Certainly, Dick Turpin is presented as morally superior to the ruling classes, who – and this has its own tradition in the penny dreadful – are invariably characterized as self-seeking, besotted fools. In Viles' account of his brief adult life, Dick Turpin spends his time rescuing damsels in distress, cutting down friends from Tyburn Tree (classic last-minute rescues), robbing the rich, and generally waging war on lecherous aristocrats, corrupt magistrates, and the poltroonish

C

[1]When **Black Bess** appeared, Robert Louis Stevenson was just thirteen years old. Perhaps he was recalling this novel twenty years later when he wrote: 'The highwayman was my favourite dish'. R. L. Stevenson, 'A Gossip on Romance', in **Longman's Magazine**, vol. 1, November 1882.

dragoons sent out to capture him, retiring now and then to some tumbledown mansion for a wild party with his fellow Knights of the Road and their ladyfriends.

The glorification of Dick Turpin (born 1705, hanged 1739) had begun in eighteenth-century broadsheets and chapbooks. The short, dumpy, balding butcher's assistant, horse-thief and robber, renowned for his brutal methods of torture, became a gay blade with magnificent moustachios, a bold and daring highwayman, a gentleman of the road, a protector of the weak and oppressed. William Harrison Ainsworth's **Rookwood,** 1843, developed the legend further, accentuating elements that appeared again and again in the dreadfuls the novel spawned (Dick's love for his horse; the fantastic ride from London to York; the accidental shooting of his accomplice Tom King). There were other celebrated highwaymen, among them Sixteen-String Jack, nicknamed thus on account of the eight silk ribbons he wore under each knee (his real name was Jack Rann, born ca. 1750, hanged 1774); and Dashing Claude Duval (born 1643, hanged 1670), renowned, the legend has it, for dancing a jig with his comely female victims.

If the highwayman stole the limelight, there were, however, other rogues as heroes in nineteenth-century popular fiction: pirates, banditti, robbers, outlaws. Ainsworth's novel about Jack Sheppard, London apprentice and gaol-breaker extraordinaire (born 1702, hanged 1724), became the sourcebook of later dreadfuls, just as Pierce Egan Jnr.'s penny-issue **Robin Hood,** 1839-40, inspired dozens of fresh accounts of life in Merrie Sherwood. Cartouche, 'the French Jack Sheppard' (real name Louis-Dominique Bourgignon, born 1693, executed 1721) appeared in England around 1860. But it was not only the criminal of the past who was immortalized in the dreadful. The crimes and death of Sheffield-born Charles Peace, porch thief, master of disguises, and murderer, were presented in penny parts within weeks of his execution in February 1879.

From yarns spun round crooks who actually existed, it was but a step to tales written about purely imaginary criminals, Charley Wags, 'boy brigands', and similar scoundrels. T. P. Prest's **String of Pearls,** serialized in a periodical in the mid-forties, detailed the crimes of a monster he called Sweeney Todd, a Fleet Street barber who used to cut his customers' throats and propel them head first into the cellar, where they were processed into 'savoury, delightful, gushing gravy pies' and sold on the adjacent premises to drooling magistrates, lawyers and clerks from the nearby law-courts. Ritchie published the first boys' version of this famous shocker in the late 1860s, an abridgement issued in his **Paragon Library.** Charles Fox commissioned G. A. Sala to rewrite Prest's novel, and **Sweeney Todd, the Demon Barber of Fleet**

Street appeared in penny parts in 1878. A story with the innocent sounding title **The Link Boy of Old London,** serialized in Fox's **Boys' Standard** in 1883, turned out to be a re-hash of Sweeney's doings. In 1892 he surfaced once more, alias Ruloff the Barber, in **The Boys of London and Boys of New York;** he may have changed his name, but he certainly had not changed his nasty habits.[2]

This account of the life, crimes, and execution of Charles Peace ran for a full two years, in 1879-80.

BIOGRAPHICAL SKETCH.

CHARLES PEACE *alias* JOHN WARD, whose life and adventures form the subject-matter of our story, has gained for himself a reputation equal, if not superior, to the lawless ruffians, Jack Sheppard, Dick Turpin, and others of a similar class. He is a union of various elements.

In more senses than one he was a local character.

No. 1.

Born in Sheffield he was, in early days, trained according to the customs of the day, and when about eight or ten years of age was one of the foremost amongst his companions in any game of audacious fun.

He was always considered a "rough," even amongst his earlier associates, and it is said that he was dreaded by the children with whom he played. At ten years of age he had to assist his father who was named

[2]For further details on the criminals and outlaws who became the heroes of popular fiction, see Victor Neuburg, **The Batsford Companion to Popular Literature,** London, 1982.

Penny-Part Novels (See also **Black Rollo, May Turpin** and **Red Ralph** under section A.)

Black Bess; or, The Knight of the Road. A Tale of the Good Old Times. London: E. Harrison, [ca. 1875]. 254 parts in 3 vols. pp. 2,028.
Originally published in 1863-68, this story, written by Edward Viles and illustrated by Robert Prowse, reputedly sold around 2 million copies in the 19th century.

The Black Highwayman. Being the Second Series of 'Black Bess.' London: E. Harrison, [ca. 1875]. 86 parts. pp. 688.
Written by Edward Viles and illustrated by Robert Prowse. Originally appeared in 1866-68.

The Black Dwarf; A Tale of Love, Mystery and Crime. Introducing Many Startling Incidents in the Life of that Celebrated Highwayman Dick Turpin. London: Hogarth House, [ca. 1880]. 36 parts in 3 vols. pp. 438.
Percy B. St. John originally wrote this novel under the pen-name Lady Esther Hope. It first appeared in 1860-61; the re-written version was issued in 1874-75.

Blueskin: A Romance of the Last Century. London: E. Harrison, [ca. 1875]. 158 parts in 2 vols. pp. 1,259.
Written by Edward Viles, illustrated by Robert Prowse and others, and first published in 1866-67.

Cartouche, the French Jack Sheppard. London: Charles Fox, [ca. 1895]. 14 parts. pp. 168.
Probably written by Walter Percy Viles; serialized in

The Boy's Standard from 16 August 1890 to 14 February 1891. Temple Publishing Co. brought out a 41-part edition ca. 1860.

Charles Peace; or, The Adventures of a Notorious Burglar. London: G. Purkess, [ca. 1879-80]. 100 parts. pp. 798.
'Founded on Fact and Profusely Illustrated.'

Charley Wag, the New Jack Sheppard. London: George Vickers, [ca. 1860-61]. 72 parts. pp. 578.
Written by G. A. Sala and illustrated by Robert Prowse.

Gentleman George, the King of the Road. London: Hogarth House, [ca. 1880]. 12 parts. pp. 118.
By J. J. G. Bradley and originally serialized in **The Boy's Standard** in 1875-76.

The Outlaws of Epping Forest. London: Hogarth House, [ca. 1880]. 25 parts. pp. 204.
First issued in penny weekly parts in 1873.

Robin Hood and the Archers of Merrie Sherwood. London: Hogarth House, [ca. 1875]. 38 parts in 3 vols. pp. 456.
Author George Emmett, illustrators Robert Prowse and Warwick Reynolds (Snr.). Originally issued under the title **Robin Hood and the Outlaws of Sherwood Forest** by the Temple Publishing Co. in 1868-69.

Sweeney Todd, the Barber of Fleet Street. A Thrilling Story of the Old City of London. Founded on Facts. London: A. Ritchie, [ca. 1868?]. pp. 16.
Issued in Ritchie's **Paragon Library.**

Sweeney Todd, the Demon Barber of Fleet Street. London: Charles Fox, [ca. 1890]. 48 parts. pp. 576.
G. A. Sala's version of this shocker (brought out by Fox in 1878) was closely based on T. P. Prest's **String of Pearls**, itself serialized in **The People's Periodical** in 1846-48, then issued in 92 penny parts in 1849-50.

Will Dudley; or, The Scarlet Riders of Hounslow Heath. London: Hogarth House, [ca. 1880]. 18 parts pp. 210.
Penned by W. L. Emmett and serialized in **The Young Briton** in 1873.

THE

BLUE DWARF;

A TALE OF

LOVE, MYSTERY, AND CRIME.

INTRODUCING

MANY STARTLING INCIDENTS IN THE LIFE OF THAT CELEBRATED HIGHWAYMAN,

DICK TURPIN.

BY PERCY B. ST. JOHN.

FULLY ILLUSTRATED BY BEAUTIFULLY EXECUTED WOOD ENGRAVINGS, SPECIALLY DRAWN FOR THIS WORK, AND FURTHER EMBELLISHED BY

TWENTY BEAUTIFUL CHROMO PICTURES,

ILLUSTRATING VARIOUS SCENES OF INTEREST DETAILED IN THE NARRATIVE.

VOLUME III.

LONDON:

HOGARTH HOUSE, BOUVERIE STREET, E.C.

Story-Papers and 'Libraries'
('Libraries' in this sense are small-format magazines
published on an irregular basis.)

Claude Duval (advertised as **Claude Duval Library**).
London: Aldine Publishing Company. Ed. by Walter Light.
48 numbers in batches of 4. [4 October 1902 to
24 March 1906].
Written by Charlton Lea. Coloured covers by
Robert Prowse, J. Arch and F. W. Boyington.

Dick Turpin (advertised as **Dick Turpin Library**).
London: Aldine Publishing Company. Ed. by Walter Light.
182 numbers in batches of 4. [5 April 1902 to
September 1909].
Written by Charlton Lea and Stephen H. Agnew.
Most of the covers by Robert Prowse, some by J. Arch and
F. W. Boyington.
18 issues were reprinted in Aldine's **Black Bess Library**,
1909-10. The texts of George Newnes' **"Black Bess"**
Library (1921-22) and his **Dick Turpin Library** (1922-30)
were re-vamped versions of Aldine's original library.

Jack Sheppard (advertised as **Jack Sheppard Library**).
London: Aldine Publishing Company. Ed. by Walter Light.
24 numbers in batches of 4. [26 November 1904 to 5 May
1906].
Coloured covers by Prowse, Arch and Boyington.

The New Newgate Calendar, Containing the Remarkable
Lives and Trials of Notorious Criminals, Past and Present.
London: Edward Harrison. 80 weekly numbers.
24 October 1863 to 6 May 1865.
Editorial comments and adverts indicate that this paper
was aimed at a teenage audience.

Robin Hood (advertised as **Robin Hood Library**).
London: Aldine Publishing Company. Ed. by Walter Light.
88 numbers in batches of 4. [19 October 1901 to
6 June 1906].
Authors: Alfred S. Burrage, C. E. Brand, Roderick Dare,
Escott Lynn [i.e. C. G. H. Lawrence], R. Mant
[i.e. G.R. M. Hearne], Singleton Pound [i.e. Oliver Merland],
H. Philpott Wright, Ogilvie Mitchell and G. C. Glover.
Illustrators: Robert Prowse and F. W. Boyington.
Undated re-issues in 1912-14 (14 nos.), 1924-27 (88 nos.)
and 1930 (8 nos.).

Rob Roy Library. London: James Henderson. 16 numbers
in batches of 4. [3 November and 22 December 1903,
23 February and 16 April 1904].
Written by Erskine Blair and Angus Maclean. Coloured
covers by Phil Ebbutt.

"Stopped by Dick Turpin!" cried King George, with an oath.
"Impossible! Why, I was informed that he was dead!" "Whoever
told you that, lied," answered Dick. "George of Hanover, surrender
your purse!"

No. 92 of **Dick Turpin** appeared on 17 March 1906; the
coloured cover was designed by Robert Prowse.

No. 64 of **Robin Hood** came out on 10 December 1904;
cover by F. W. Boyington.

ONE PENNY

ROBIN HOOD

64

FOR ENGLAND'S SAKE

"Are ye for the King?" shouted Grissel. "Ay, ay!" shouted the villagers. "We are for the Lion-Heart!" "Then stay your hands, ye know not whom ye would slay, for this is Robin Hood!" The smith paused and his comrades stood still. Then Robin stepped forward. "I am Robin Hood," he said.

READY ON THURSDAY NEXT, APRIL 14.   ONE PENNY WEEKLY.

24 Pages of Sensational Romance,

IN HANDSOME COLOURED WRAPPER.

ORDER AT ONCE.   NOS. **1 & 2** OF   ORDER AT ONCE.

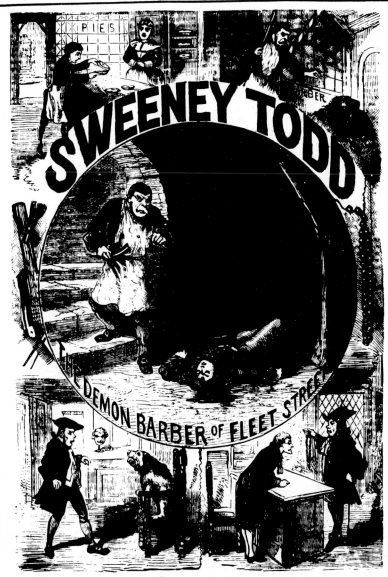

A Magnificent Coloured Picture Given Away with Nos. 1 & 2.

A Magnificent Coloured Picture Given Away with Nos. 1 & 2.

Another Splendid Picture Given Away with No. 3.

LONDON : CHARLES FOX, 4, Shoe-lane, Fleet Street, E.C., and all Newsagents.

Printed by SULLY and FORD, Plough-court, Fetter-lane E.C., and Published by CHARLES FOX, the Proprietor, at 4, Shoe-lane, Fleet-street, London, E.C.

DIME NOVELS

The house of Beadle & Adams, founded in 1860, pioneered the publication of dime novels in the States, the counterparts in quality and public esteem of British penny dreafuls. It seemed tempting to reprint this material in Britain; after all, it had been tried on the market, and, as purveyors of cheap fiction generally adopted a cavalier attitude towards copyright, no further payment of authors or illustrators would be incurred. However, recent study of the ledgers of the foremost of the reprint firms, the Aldine Publishing Company, has shown that the profits were very slight; indeed, Aldine made a loss for practically every year of its existence![1] The ruthless way the texts were maltreated in that literary abattoir must have been a contributory factor, a dime novel being butchered to fit in the **"O'er Land and Sea" Library** (1890), chopped up again and given a new title for the **Half-Holiday Library** (1892), then mutilated further and served up with a different title in the **Cheerful Library** (1894). (On display is a volume of the **Cheerful Library** from the publisher's archives which shows how the editor set about his work.) The texts may have been indigestible and the print shoddy, but the youngster who paid a penny for a copy of the **Boys' First-Rate Pocket Library** (1887) or the **Invention, Travel & Adventure Library** (1890) no doubt savoured the brightly coloured covers which were to become Aldine's trademark and which have made its penny booklets collectors' items today. Both gripping title and lurid cover pledged something not always fulfilled in the stories themselves (not that this was an unusual feature of cheap fiction at this time). The purchaser of **Deadwood Dick's Head Off,** 1894, would have been forgiven for fearing that the crime-buster's career had been abruptly terminated, but it just so happens that the head rolling across the prairie belongs to some minor dispensable character, and that huge gleaming traction engine on the cover, which seems to have perpetrated the beheading, has precious little to do with the tale.

Deadwood Dick, one of the heroes of the **Boys' First-Rate Pocket Library,** started off his fictional career as a trapper and outlaw in the Black Hills of South Dakota, but after his moral conversion – or rather, after post office action in the States against publishers of dime novels – he became a dispenser of rough border justice, finally a detective. Aldine introduced many colourful characters from the mythical Wild West into Britain, including Antelope Abe, Bonanza Bill, Captain Cactus, Denver Doll and so on through the alphabet. A young, conceited, impecunious border scout by the name of William F. Cody was elevated to folk-hero in 1869 in **Buffalo Bill, the King of the Border Men** by Ned Buntline (pen-name of Edward Zane Carroll Judson), and the saga was continued by Colonel Prentiss Ingraham. Buffalo Bill first appeared in Britain in one of Brett's story-papers before

D

[1] W. O. G. Lofts, 'Success and Failure: A short History of English "Penny Dreadful" Publishers', in **Dime Novel Roundup**, no. 523, February 1977.

coming in person with his Wild West Show, prompting Purkess, Aldine, Henderson, Strong and Harmsworth to jump on the bandwagon and publish yarns about his fantastic frontier feats.

The American cowboy was a far more popular figure in Britain than the American detective. The sleuth Nick Carter had quite a European following, but despite mopping up nihilists, unmasking imposters, and tracking down diamond thieves in a number of English story-papers, he never quite made an inroad into the corner of the market securely occupied by Sexton Blake and Nelson Lee.[2] **The Boys of London and Boys of New York,** a boys' paper which consisted of reprints from Norman L. Munro's **Our Boys** and **Boys of New York,** and Frank Tousey and George G. Small's **Young Men of America,** regularly featured an American sleuth nicknamed Old King Brady, who had first appeared in 1883 in the USA in a story called **99 99th Street. The Boys of London and Boys of New York,** described by the **Quarterly Review** in 1890 as 'a shabby and ill-printed rag', also contained westerns, rags-to-riches stories, and yarns about the exploits of a young inventor, Frank Reade.

Frank Reade was the creation of Harry Enton, but after three episodes the series was taken over by 'Noname' (i.e. Luis P. Senarens). The stories originally appeared in the **Boys of New York** and the **Wide Awake Library.** In England it was the Aldine Publishing Company which systematically exploited this rich seam in the dime novel, reprinting the adventures in its **Invention, Travel & Adventure Library.** Most of the stories actually starred the inventor's equally inventive son Frank Reade Junior. The boy's first invention was a steam-driven robot.[3] With smoke streaming out of his top-hat-cum-funnel, the Steam Man used to stomp through the plains at 40 m.p.h. chasing Comanches and then trampling them underfoot. Apparently the Steam Man could only move forwards. This and the fact that he was equipped with an inefficient braking system led to his demise; approaching a cliff one day he jogged straight into it and exploded. Undaunted, Frank Reade cheerfully set to work on an even more powerful engine, a Steam Horse, followed by two robots he called his Steam Team. Unperturbed by their self-destruction, Frank returned to his lab in the desert to work feverishly on a more ambitious and up-to-date project. It was after all the age of Faraday and Bell, and Frank's new machines ran on electricity, with motors far more sophisticated and weaponry far more deadly than their unimaginative names suggested: Electric Canoe, Electric Fish, Electric Bird, and Electric Tricycle. The illustrator must have thrown up his hands in dismay at the mock-scientific explanation that these vessels were driven by 'electric dynamos and

[2]Nick Carter appeared in **Comic Life** in 1904; **The Boy's Peep Show,** 1905; **The Aldine Half-Holiday Library,** 1906; **The Aldine Cheerful Library,** 1910; Newnes's **Nick Carter Weekly** in 1911-12 and his **Nick Carter Library,** 1918-20.
[3]The idea was borrowed from E. S. Ellis, **The Steam Man of the Praire,** published by Beadle & Adams in 1865. Aldine reprinted this as **The Iron Hunter** in 1887.

suspensory rotascopes'; commissioned to draw the electric plane, he produced something like a cross between a bird, a bat, a mediaeval castle, and a machine-gun turret. Such was the quality of the futuristic tales in the **Invention, Travel & Adventure Library,** a title to which some wag in the Aldine office added the regular sub-title 'Jules Verne Outdone!!!'

The Aldine "Boys' First-Rate Pocket Library" of Complete Tales. London: Aldine Publishing Company. 472 nos. [1887 to 1905].
Initial circulation 80,000 copies; in 1897 just 40,000.

The Aldine Cheerful Library. The Most Popular Complete Weekly. London: Aldine Publishing Company.
1st series: 76 nos; 17 February 1894 to 31 July 1895.
2nd series: 822 nos; 7 August 1895 to 29 April 1911.
3rd series: 27 nos; 6 May to 4 November 1911.

The Aldine Half-Holiday Library. A Complete Story of Adventure Weekly. London: Aldine Publishing Company. 904 nos. 6 September 1892 to 13 January 1910.

The Aldine "O'er Land and Sea" Library. London: Amalgamated Press. 408 issues. [1890 to 1905].

The Aldine Romance of Invention, Travel & Adventure Library, Jules Verne Outdone!!! London: Aldine Publishing Company. 272 nos. [1894 to 1906].
Cheap reprint as **The Invention Library** in 1910-12 (32 nos.) and 1913 (12 nos.).

The Boys of London and Boys of New York. London: James Jackson/Henry Wells Jackson. 1,219 issues. 1 June 1877 to 15 September 1900.

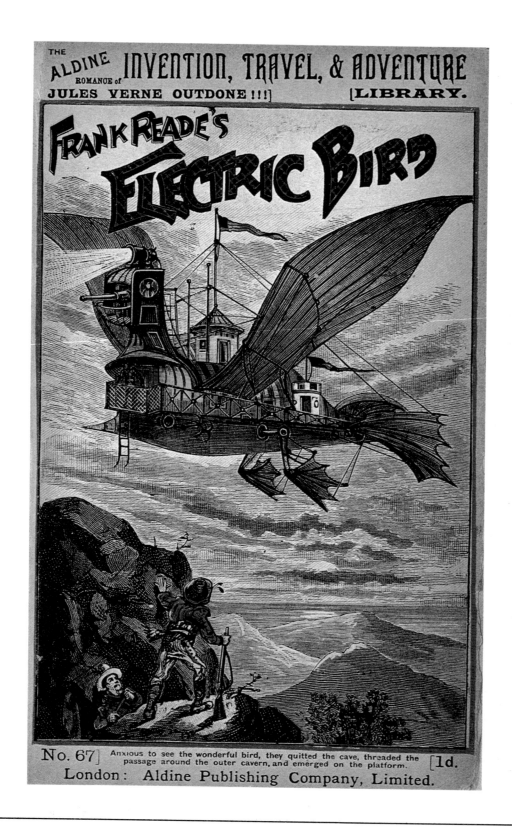

THE
ALDINE INVENTION, TRAVEL, & ADVENTURE
ROMANCE of
JULES VERNE OUTDONE !!!] [LIBRARY.

FRANK READE'S ELECTRIC BIRD

No. 67] Anxious to see the wonderful bird, they quitted the cave, threaded the passage around the outer cavern, and emerged on the platform. [1d.

London: Aldine Publishing Company, Limited.

Dime novels from the States found their way into England
in the late-nineteenth century via the Aldine Publishing
Company.

B.O.P., G.O.P., AND 'HEALTHY READING FOR THE YOUNG'

Samuel O. Beeton's **Boys' Own Magazine** (1855) was certainly not the first periodical produced for children in affluent families – the earliest juvenile periodicals date back to the mid-eighteenth century – but it was the first boys' magazine to shift its main emphasis from teaching towards amusement. The original recipe of Beeton's monthly embraced a balanced mixture of informative articles on natural history, potted biographies of famous men, brief pieces on famous places, weapons, sport and pastimes, and puzzles, poems and competitions. The first yearly volume, which contained no fiction at all, won 10,000 subscribers. Nevertheless, it would not have become a commercial success, for which treble this circulation was required, if Beeton had not added the new category 'Tales and Adventures'. He began by printing Edgar Allan Poe's **The Gold-Beetle** (better known as **The Gold Bug**), then short stories by Friedrick Gerstaecker, later full-length novels by W. H. G. Kingston and Mayne Reid. As a result, circulation rose to 40,000 copies per month.[1] In the early 1860s, Beeton and the young author John George Edgar drew up a plan to present the history of England in a series of novels to be serialised in **The Boys' Own Magazine** before being issued in cloth-bound form. Edgar died suddenly in 1864 after completing four of these stories, but he had already laid the foundations of the historical novel for children.

Beeton had pioneered the monthly magazine for boys of the middle and upper-middle classes (at 6d a copy his periodical was way beyond the pocket of a worker's son), and there were soon other publishers keen to follow in his footsteps. Edmund Routledge, the nineteen-year-old son of the respected publisher George Routledge, was one of those who thought the market could sustain another monthly and his **Every Boy's Magazine** appeared in February 1862. Tweedie's **Young England** also began in 1862, and the following year **The Boys' Journal** appeared, edited by C. P. Brown, containing fiction by some of the most competent boys' writers of this era. Hodder and Stoughton joined in the scramble for boys' pocket-money in 1865 with their **Merry and Wise,** aimed at a slightly younger age-group than the others. All this competition was too fierce for Beeton and he went bankrupt in 1866. Ward, Lock & Co. bought up his stock and the name of his periodical, which continued to appear under their imprint until 1874.

The magazines mentioned above were all relatively expensive and were all issued at monthly intervals, although the purveyors of penny dreadfuls had already proved that there was a far wider audience for cheaper weekly papers. From 1866, the respectable publishing houses increasingly turned their attention to a wider public, producing alternatives to what was considered objectionable cheap fiction. **Chatterbox** (1866) was founded by Rev. Erskine J. Clarke to combat the blood-and-thunder literature he thought was depraving the youth of his day; it was beamed at a

[1]Circulation figures from Sheila Egoff, **Children's Periodicals of the Nineteenth Century**, London, 1951 (Library Association Pamphlets, no. 8).

young audience, so as to channel their interests into the approved directions right from the start. The most successful of these penny weeklies put out by the established publishing houses banished direct moralising from their pages, reducing the informative articles to a few snippets, and heavily emphasizing fiction. **Young Folks** (1871) specialised in fairy tales (the King Pippin series by Roland Quiz, pen-name of R. M. H. Quittenton) and exciting adventure stories, including Stevenson's **Treasure Island** (1881-82), **The Black Arrow** (1883), and his **Kidnapped** (1886). **The Union Jack** (1880), announcing that it would contain 'Healthy, Stirring Tales of Adventures by Land and Sea', went a little too far and consisted exclusively of serials by Kingston, Henty, Verne and others. The policy of printing nothing but fiction did not pay and in 1883 this paper was discontinued.

As there were many story-papers to choose in the 1890s, beginning a new one was something of a risk. **Chums** (1892), published by Cassell & Co., did not do at all well until it began to include thrilling pirate stories by Samuel Walkey; in the expansionist late nineties it turned into a paper with a strong pro-Empire line in both its fiction and non-fiction departments. Amongst all these papers aimed at boys from both ordinary and well-to-do families, there was one which was to become something of a national institution, and was affectionately known simply by its initial letters, **B.O.P. The Boys' Own Paper** (1879) had the highest circulation of any boys' paper in the Victorian age, and most recognized writers and illustrators at some time contributed to it, making it 'the most important and influential children's periodical ever to have appeared in Britain.'[2]

B.O.P. was published by the Religious Tract Society with the avowed aim of weaning boys away from their penny dreadfuls by providing a fare of 'sound and healthy reading' for them. Whilst the paper was still at the planning stage, its editor, G. A. Hutchison, had repeatedly clashed with the R.T.S. directors, who wanted yet another pious periodical, and one after the other a series of specimen issues was rejected until approval was finally given. The main bone of contention was Hutchison's insistence on a strong emphasis on fiction. He argued that boys would no longer touch the old kind of moralistic magazines, but would eagerly devour a story-paper; and that admirable behaviour, and values of honesty, industry and perseverence could be skilfully embedded in fiction in such a way as to be palatable to children. The new boys' paper had, after all, to face stiff competition from a lively trade in cheap literature. Only after heated altercation in the General Literature Committee of the R.T.S. was Hutchison's idea of a story-paper that would fight fire with fire finally accepted. When **The Boys' Own Paper** appeared in mid-January 1879 it was sold out within three days. To make sure that boys of the lower classes heard about it right from the start, thousands of copies were distributed in London's Board schools.

[2]Patrick A. Dunae, '**The Boys' Own Paper**: Origins and Editorial Policies', in **The Private Library**, vol. 9, winter 1976.

The first pages of **B.O.P.** were given over to an anonymous short story called 'My First Football Match' (for 'football' read rugby). On one level the story was about a youngster's brilliant first game in the school team; on a deeper level it was about his initiation into the code of behaviour of an élite. It was no accident that the qualities informing this story–courage, determination, team spirit – were presented in the context of the playing-field of a public school. This coincided with the late-Victorian belief in the crucial role of sport in the process of building character and forming a proper understanding of team spirit and leadership. Talbot Baines Reed, the author of 'My First Football Match', later contributed a series of full-length school stories to **B.O.P.,** including the well-known **Fifth Form at St. Dominic's** in 1881-82. Reed refashioned the school story, breaking completely with the morbid and lachrymose **Eric** tradition, and establishing a new tradition in atmosphere, ethics, characters, and plot.[3]

The young reader of the first issue of **B.O.P.** also discovered the opening chapters of an adventure serial by that doyen of boys' fiction W. H. G. Kingston. A naval story set at the time of the wars against the French, **From Powder Monkey to Admiral** depicted the progress of a highly improbable career; in a later preface to the book, Dr. James Macaulay (the supervising editor of **The Boys' Own Paper**) defended the novel in these words:

> "While it is true that no sailor boy may now hope to become Admiral of the Fleet, yet there is room for advancement, in peace as in war, to what is better than mere rank or title or wealth, a position of honour and usefulness. Good character and good conduct, pluck and patience, steadiness and application, will win their way, whether on sea or land, and in every calling."

Among the other writers of adventure stories for **B.O.P.** were R. M. Ballantyne, G. A. Henty, G. M. Fenn, David Ker, and hundreds more, writers who shared a belief that fiction was not merely there for entertainment, but was a means of educating boys to become tough and patriotic young men. Many of their serialized novels were set in far-flung corners of the Empire where might was right, duty was duty, and native unrest was put down by the application of 'the glorious British uppercut' coupled with the glorious English Maxim gun. The violence and killing characteristic of the penny dreadful seem to have been perfectly acceptable in an imperial context.

If fiction was the dominant element in **The Boys' Own Paper,** it was certainly not the only one. From the start each issue had a variety of material on hobbies, sport, nature, and a popular section 'Health Hints for Growing Boys', in which the eccentric Dr. Stables dispensed stern advice to his adolescent correspondents. His famous and oft-repeated recommendation to boys suffering from what the

[3]See Patrick Howarth, **Play Up and Play the Game,** London, 1973, chapter 3.

Victorians called 'nervousness' was that they should 'Take a cold tub, sir!' This phrase was used in 1982 as the title of a history of **B.O.P.** written by its last editor, Jack Cox.

And what did girls in middle-class families read towards the end of the nineteenth century? In his article on girls' reading, Edward Salmon presented an impressive list of names of women writing fiction for girls, adding reflectively that their books were not well received[1] Neither an idealized picture of womanhood nor the domestic reality lent itself easily to exciting fiction, so older girls generally read the same novels as their mothers, whilst younger girls read their brothers' adventure books and papers. There were, in fact, only three girls' periodicals acceptable to middle-class families at this time. **The Monthly Packet** (1851) had been founded to provide elevating reading for the 'steadfast and dutiful daughters of our beloved Catholic Church.' The soberly bound 97 volumes promise little light entertainment, although some fiction did appear in its pages (Charlotte Yonge's **Daisy Chain,** for instance, in 1853-55). **Every Girl's Magazine** (1878) was basically a collection of practical tips for the household and had a very limited circulation. Finally, there was the **Girls' Own Paper** (1880), devised as companion to **The Boys' Own Paper,** although never quite reaching its circulation or status. The only periodical read with any enthusiasm by girls in well-to-do families, **G.O.P.** was certainly more liberal in its philosophy of life than the following extract from the prospectus for volume one suggests;

"This magazine will aim at being to the girls a Counsellor, Playmate, Guardian, Instructor, Companion and Friend. It will help train them in moral and domestic virtues, preparing them for the responsibilities of womanhood and for a heavenly home."

[1] Edward Salmon, 'What Girls Read', in **The Nineteenth Century**, vol. 20, October 1886.

Every Boy's Magazine (1862-64)/Routledge's Magazine for Boys (1865-68)/The Young Gentleman's Magazine (1869-73)/Every Boy's Magazine (1874-88). London: Routledge & Warne/George Routledge & Sons. Ed. by Edmund Routledge. 320 monthly parts. February 1862 to September 1888.
Yearly vols. as Every Boy's Annual or Routledge's Every Boy's Annual.

The Girl's Own Paper (1880-1908)/The Girl's Own Paper and Woman's Magazine (1908-27)/Woman's Magazine and Girl's Own Paper (1927-30)/The Girl's Own Paper (1931)/The Girl's Own Paper Heiress (1941-50)/The Heiress (1950-56).
The first series was published by the Religious Tract Society and edited by Charles Peters. It appeared in approx. 1,500 weekly nos. from 3 January 1880 to 26 September 1908. Yearly volumes (29) as The Girl's Own Annual.
Circulation in the 19th century approx. 250,000 copies p.w.

Little Folks, A Magazine for the Young. London: Cassell & Co./Amalgamated Press. Ed. by Bonavia Hunt and Clara Matéaux (1871-75)/George Weatherly (1875-80)/Ernest Foster (1880-94)/Sam H. Hamer. 800 weekly nos. January 1871 to February 1933.

Merry and Wise (1865-70)/Old Merry's Monthly (1871-72). London: Jackson, Walford & Hodder/Hodder & Stoughton (from 1869). Ed. by 'Old Merry' [i.e. Edwin Hodder]. 96 monthly parts. January 1865 to December 1872.
Yearly volumes as Old Merry's Annual. Title presumably from the old song It is Good to be Merry and Wise.

The Monthly Packet (original title The Monthly Packet of Evening Readings for Younger Members of the English Church). London: John & Charles Mozley/Mozely & Smith/Walter Smith/Walter Smith & Innes/A. D. Innes & Co. Ed. by Charlotte M. Yonge, 1851-93 (with Christabel R. Coleridge, 1891-93)/C. R. Coleridge and Arthur Innes, 1893-99.
1st series: 180 monthly parts in 30 vols.; January 1851 to December 1865.
2nd series: 180 monthly parts in 30 vols.; January 1866 to December 1880.
3rd series: 120 monthly parts in 20 vols.; January 1881 to December 1890.
4th series: 100 monthly parts in 17 vols.; January 1891 to June 1899.

The Union Jack, A Magazine of Healthy, Stirring Tales of Adventure by Land and Sea. London: Griffith & Farran/Cecil Brooks/Sampson, Marston, Searle & Rivington. Ed. by W. H. G. Kingston (1880)/G. A. Henty (1880-82)/G. A. Henty and Bernard Heldmann (1882-83). 191 nos. in 4 vols. 1 January 1880 to 25 September 1883.
Circulation did not rise above 30,000 copies p.w.

Young England. London: W. Tweedie. 48 monthly parts in 4 vols. 1 January 1862 to 1 December 1865.

Young England, An Illustrated Magazine for Boys Throughout the English-Speaking World. London: Sunday School Union/Melrose. Ed. by Benjamin Clarke/Thomas Archer/H. G. Croser.
Approx. 260 weekly nos. followed by approx. 640 monthly parts. 3 January 1880 to 1937.
The continuation of Kind Words for Boys and Girls (1866-79).
Appeared simultaneously with a supplement under the title The B.B. (i.e. Boys' Brigade).

Young Folks. Our Young Folks' Weekly Budget (1871-76)/Young Folks' Weekly Budget (1879)/Young Folks (1879-84)/Young Folks' Paper (1884-91)/Old and Young (1891-96)/Folks at Home (1896-97). London: James Henderson. Ed. by James Henderson/S. Holland/Robert Leighton/Roland Quiz [i.e. R. M. H. Quittenton]/Charles A. Read. 1,380 nos. 2 January 1871 to 29 April 1897.
A specimen number was given away with the Weekly Budget dated 24 December 1870.

Aunt Judy's Magazine. London: Bell & Daldy (1866)/George Bell & Sons (1866-81)/Messrs. Allen (1881-82)/Bemrose & Sons (1882-84)/Hatchards (1884-85). Ed. by Mrs. Alfred Gatty (1866-74)/H. K. F. Gatty & Juliana Ewing (1874-76)/H. K. F. Gatty (1877-85). 238 monthly parts in 22 vols. January 1866 to October 1885.
Yearly vols. as Aunt Judy's Christmas Volume/Aunt Judy's Annual Volume.
Juliana Ewing was nicknamed 'Aunt Judy' by her younger brothers and sisters to whom she first told her stories.

The Boys' Journal, A Magazine of Literature, Science, Adventure, and Amusement. London: Henry Vickers. Ed. by Charles Perry Brown. 98 monthly parts in 11 vols. January 1863 to February 1871.

The Boy's Own Magazine. London: Samuel O. Beeton (to 1866)/Ward, Lock & Co. Ed. by S. O. Beeton.
1st series: 96 monthly nos.; January 1855 to December 1862.
2nd series: 84 monthly nos.; January 1863 to December 1869.
3rd series: 60 monthly nos.; January 1870 to December 1874.
Initial circulation 10,000 copies per month, by 1863 approx. 40,000.
The 1st and 2nd series appeared in yearly volumes as The Boy's Own Magazine/The Boy's Own Volume/Beeton's Boy's Annual. The 3rd series appeared in yearly and half-yearly volumes under varying titles (e.g. vol. 3 appeared as Beeton's Brave Tales, Bold Ballads, and Travels and Perils by Land and Sea).
A reprint, Beeton's Boy's Own Magazine, edited by G. A. Henty and issued by Ward & Lock, ran to 23 monthly nos. from January 1889 to November 1890. These 6 vols. were bound as Beeton's Boy's Own Magazine (New Series), and also appeared under different titles (vol. 1 as Stories of Land and Sea).

The Boy's Own Paper. London: Religious Tract Society (originally as the "Leisure Hour" Office)/Lutterworth Press (from 1939)/Purnell & Sons (from 1963). Ed. by George Alfred Hutchinson (1879-1912)/Arthur Lincoln Haydon (1912-24)/Geoffrey Richard Pocklington (1924-33)/George J. H. Northcroft (1933-35)/Robert Harding (1935-42)/Leonard Halls (1942-46)/Jack Cox (1946-67). 1,767 weekly nos. from 18 January 1879 to 28 September 1914, thereafter approx. 650 monthly parts from October 1914 to February 1967.
Yearly vols. as **The Boy's Own Annual.** These annuals continued to appear until 1979.
The first volume of the **B.O.P.** appeared under the nominal editorship of Dr. James Macaulay.
Approx. 200,000 copies in 1879; 500,000 copies in the 80s; 650,000 copies in the 90s; 400,000 from 1900 to 1914. In 1967 just 20,000 copies per month.

The Captain, A Magazine for Boys and Old Boys. London: George Newnes. Ed. by 'The Old Fag' (Robert Stanley Warren Bell up to 1910). 300 monthly issues in 50 vols. April 1899 to March 1924.

BRAVE AND TRUE.

WHATEVER you are, be brave, boys !
    The liar's a coward and slave, boys !
      Though clever at ruses,
      And sharp at excuses,
He's a sneaking and pitiful knave, boys.

Whatever you are, be frank, boys !
'Tis better than money and rank, boys :
      Still cleave to the right,
      Be lovers of light,
Be open, above board, and frank, boys.

Whatever you are, be kind, boys !
Be gentle in manners and mind, boys !
      The man gentle in mien,
      Words, and temper, I ween,
Is the gentleman truly refined, boys.

But, whatever you are, be true, boys !
Be visible through and through, boys :
      Leave to others the shamming,
      The "greening" and "cramming,"
In fun and in earnest, be true, boys !

            HENRY DOWNTON.

Chatterbox. London: William Macintosh/Wells Gardner, Darton & Co./Simpkin, Marshall & Co./Dean. Ed. by Rev. J. Erskine Clarke/William J. Harvey Darton (1901-31). A weekly, beginning 1 December 1866, Then a monthly, finally an annual from 1946 to 1955.

The Child's Companion, The Penny Monthly for Boys and Girls of 6 to 16 Years of Age. London: Religious Tract Society. Approx. 1,310 monthly issues from 1824 to 1932.

Chums. London: Cassell & Co./Amalgamated Press. Ed. by Max Pemberton (1892-93)/Ernest Foster (1894-1907)/E. H. Robinson (1907-15)/ F. Knowles Camping (1915-18)/ A. Donnelly Aitken (1918-20)/Clarence Winchester (1920-24)/Arthur L. Hayward (1924-26)/Draycott M. Dell (1926-34). 2,077 issues. 14 September 1892 to 2 July 1932. Cassell brought out 33 annuals (1892-1925), A. P. a further 15 (1926-41).

PRICE ONE PENNY.] **FIRST NUMBER OF A NEW VOLUME.**
With Presentation Plate in Colours—"A Struggle to the Death."

CHUMS

No. 311.—Vol. VII.]   AUGUST 24, 1898.   [ALL RIGHTS RESERVED.

"THE TRUMPETER SPEARED HIS MEN AS THEY STOOD." (*See page* 2.)

Chums presented colonial life as exciting and dangerous. This account of how a courageous young trooper won the V.C. in Afghanistan was illustrated by Paul Hardy.

This exhortative poem appeared in the first issue of **B.O.P.**, 18 January 1879.

The Boy's Own Paper, which ran from 1879 to 1967, was originally published by the Religious Tract Society as an antidote to the penny dreadful. The masthead was designed and engraved by Edward Whymper.

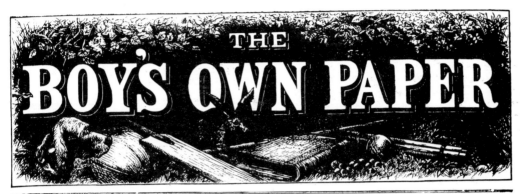

THE BOY'S OWN PAPER

No. 1.—Vol. I.   SATURDAY, JANUARY 18, 1879.   Price One Penny. [ALL RIGHTS RESERVED.

MY FIRST FOOTBALL MATCH.

By an Old Boy.

IT was a proud moment in my existence when Wright, captain of our football club, came up to me in school one Friday and said, "Adams, your name is down to play in the match against Craven to-morrow."

I could have knighted him on the spot. To be one of the picked "fifteen," whose glory it was to fight the battles of their school in the Great Close, had been the leading ambition of my life—I suppose I ought to be ashamed to confess it—ever since, as a little chap of ten, I entered Parkhurst six years ago. Not a winter Saturday but had seen me either looking on at some big match, or oftener still scrimmaging about with a score or so of other juniors in a scratch game. But for a long time, do what I would, I always

seemed as far as ever from the coveted goal, and was half despairing of ever rising to win my "first fifteen cap." Latterly, however, I had noticed Wright and a few others of our best players more than once lounging about in the Little Close where we juniors used to play, evidently taking observations with an eye to business. Under the awful gaze of these heroes, need I say I exerted myself as I had never done before? What cared I for hacks or bruises, so only that I could distinguish myself in their eyes? And never was music sweeter

"Down!"

VOL. I.—No. 1.]　　　　　　　JANUARY 3, 1880.　　　　　　　[PRICE ONE PENNY.

ZARA:
OR, MY GRANDDAUGHTER'S MONEY.

CHAPTER I.
AN ARRIVAL.

THE streets of a dreary London suburb were more dreary than usual on that December evening. A dense fog was fast gathering up its yellow vapour, making the shabby, tumble-down region only one degree less obscure than it would be at midnight. Jasper Meade, proprietor of the "Commercial Lodging House," stood on his own door-step, whistling a dismal refrain very much out of tune, but at the moment he was not thinking of melody — his keen, restless black eyes were striving to penetrate the mist. He watched every vehicle that rattled past, splashing through the sloppy mud, waking up the echoes for a short space, and disappearing into the obscurity beyond, and considered it another lost chance, a fresh disappointment. The secret of this was that Jasper's last venture in the world of speculation was not realising his expectations.

He had lately purchased the lodging-house before-mentioned, and found his venture was of questionable advantage. It had been described in the advertisement as "ruinously cheap," having

"WILL YOU COME TO MY LITTLE ROOM?"

spacious, well-furnished rooms, good stables, every convenience for man and beast, and doing a splendid business. Tempted by the delusive bait, he had rashly invested the whole of his capital in the purchase, awakening too late to the knowledge that much gloss and rosy tint is apt to be used in advertising, and that a bargain rarely comes up to the description given of its merits.

Rooms, many and various, there certainly were in the old house, but they looked as though generations of bygone travellers had tarried there, disported themselves without restraint, and then gone on their ways. The walls were sullied and grimy, the furniture worn out, the carpets ragged and faded, the whole place disreputable in the extreme. Jasper's wife — a pretty, bright-eyed little woman, charming with her Frenchified manner, born and bred a lady had been driven to utter despair when Jasper took her down to that suburban establishment, and told her it was to be their future home! The meanness and vulgarity of the place were repugnant to Phillis; every instinct of her nature revolted, she

Routledge's Every Boy's Annual for 1875 contained Jules Verne's novel **Captain Grant.**

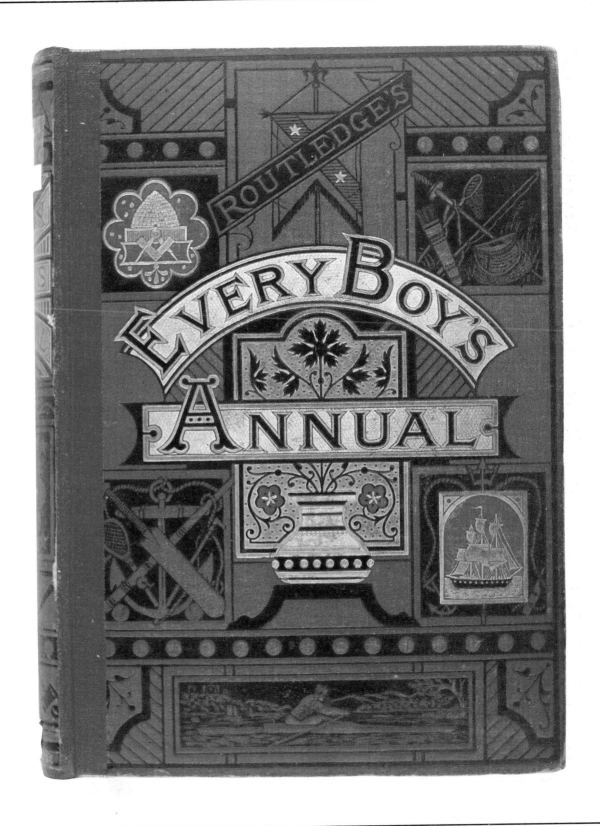

HARMSWORTH'S CRUSADE AGAINST THE PENNY DREADFUL

Alfred Harmsworth had already published **Answers** (1888) and a series of successful comics (see section J) before he declared war on the penny dreadful. In the nineties he brought out a number of story-papers for boys – **Marvel** (1893), **Union Jack** (1894), **Pluck** (1894) and **The Boys' Friend** (1895) – all of which, he repeatedly claimed, were 'Started to Suppress Bad Books for Boys'. For nearly a decade, virtually every issue would contain some scathing reference to the baneful influence of the 'penny horribles'. In the editorials, warning tales were related about errand boys who, after an overdose of sub-literary trash, chloroformed their bosses, pilfered the petty cash, and attempted to make their getaway to the States in rowing boats. In addition, every issue contained some testimonial, whether a statement by a metropolitan magistrate or a young railway clerk's letter, lauding the clean, pure fiction put out by Harmsworth.

An article in the first number of **The Boys' Friend** conveniently summarizes all the objections made against the penny dreadful.[1] The writers were 'miserable beer-swilling wretches' who wrote their drivelling stories in the seediest of lodging-houses; the printers used old type and the cheapest paper available; the publishers made a mint out of reprints and shoddy, pernicious literature; the boy readers were invariably led into a life of degredation and crime. It would not be too difficult to prove that this was a case of the pot calling the kettle black. The paper and print in Harmsworth's papers were scarcely any better; his writers (such as H. S. Warwick and E. H. Burrage) were often recruited from the publishers he scorned; and may readers and parents could frankly see little difference between his serials and the penny horribles. Harmsworth's papers, to his intense annoyance, were themselves branded penny dreadfuls.[2]

The war he was waging with such ferocity was less a crusade based on moral conviction than a campaign embarked on for commercial reasons. By the end of the century Harmsworth had defeated his 'enemies', that is, his competitors in the publishing trade. **Boys of England** closed down in 1899, by which time most of the small publishers of boys' periodicals had been forced to the wall. Two of the weapons Harmsworth had used effectively were advertising in his other magazines and newspapers, and, more devastatingly, the startlingly low price of his boys' papers, sold in the nineties for ha'penny each.

The price of Harmsworth's story-papers was, however, not the only factor in their success. His publications were emphatically up-to-date, reflecting hectic life in a hectic decade, whereas his main rival E. J. Brett's papers had changed little over

---

[1] The "Penny Dreadful" And The Scoundrels Who Write It', in **The Boys' Friend** dated 29 January 1895. For an account of the precarious lives led by boys' writers at the turn of the century, see T. C. Bridges, **Florida to Fleet Street**, London, [1926].

[2] See, for example, the first few pages of James Joyce's story 'An Encounter' (set in the mid-nineties) in his **Dubliners**, 1914.

thirty years. Above all, it was attitudes to the Empire which separated the old from the new. For Brett, the Empire had never been more than a colourful backcloth to the wild and wonderful fiction his hacks produced. Harmsworth's **Pluck,** with its emphasis on the deeds and bravery of the men who had laid the foundations of the Empire, and those who were still busy expanding its borders, and with its plea for a course of Empire-related studies and cadet training for all boys, was an efficient mouthpiece for the jingoism of the age. By the nineties, **Boys of England** had become dull and old-fashioned; the **Pluck** group were new, smart, exciting and eager to tell boys all about the world at their feet. While Brett's papers had become increasingly impersonal, Harmsworth also appreciated the value of a chummy atmosphere in his periodicals, recognising the crucial function of the editor as mediator between reader and publisher.

Hamilton Edwards, who edited the companion papers **The Boys' Friend** (1895), **The Boys' Realm** (1902) and **The Boys' Herald** (1905), often dwelt on the way he saw his role as editor. He regarded himself as a true friend to his readers, a friend who had seen much of the world and was thus in a position to dispense sound advice. Without being paternalistic, he was someone boys could always turn to for sympathy, help or encouragement. He understood the enthusiasms of youth but, as a responsible adult, felt it his duty to channel their high spirits. In 1909 Edwards proclaimed in a 'special message' that he felt his relationship to his readers was a 'mystic fellowship', where his selfless efforts as editor were reflected in the readers' steadfast loyalty to his papers. The only way such loyalty could be expressed, of course, was through a subscription. The real character of the page of Editor's Chat is revealed in the sheer quantity of thinly disguised adverts for other Harmsworth publications it contained, as well as repeated exhortations to readers to win new converts. Boys were urged to send in postcards detailing their favourite serials; and even the competitions were organized in such a way as to provide useful data for market research. There was nothing terribly mystical about that.

To begin with, the stories in the Harmsworth boys' papers were traditional. **Marvel** specialized in journeys in search of buried treasure; the **Union Jack** was decorated with the usual trappings of adventure fiction (pirates, Redskins, desert islands, monsters of the deep, etc.); **Pluck** had a penchant for daring deeds in an Empire setting, particularly Afghanistan, India and Egypt. In the late nineties Africa became a popular stage for the adventures of diamond seekers (who often stumbled across something far more precious, a white-skinned queen) and for re-runs of recent military conflicts (the Matabele, Zulu and Boer Wars). War was brought nearer home towards the end of the century in a spate of invasion stories presenting the attempts by France, Germany and Russia, alone or in collusion, to catch Britain unawares, steaming in from the continent, sneaking through the Channel Tunnel, or floating in on Zeppelins. In **Britain in Arms** (1895), the French

and Russians are repelled by the 17th Lancers ('The Death-or-Glory Boys'); later stories increasingly featured German attempts to take Britain by storm.

Gradually, the penny dreadful heroes crept in through the back door, and only the naivest reader could have swallowed the claim that this fiction was not 'blood-and-thunder trash by vulgar scribblers but true stories of real life written with great moderation by well-respected writers'. Buffalo Bill returned as early as 1895; he was soon followed by the highwaymen, then Jack Sheppard, and Robin Hood. The nortorious burglar Charles Peace, (see section C) appeared in 1904. The same year E. H. Burrage, author of such classic dreadfuls as **Broad-Arrow Jack** (see section B), revived those popular characters Handsome Harry and Ching-Ching for **The Boys' Realm.** There was evidently some truth in A. A. Milne's remark that 'Harmsworth killed the "penny dreadful" by the simple process of producing the ha'penny dreadfuller.'

Harmsworth's halfpenny boys' magazines swept the penny dreadful off the market in the 1890s. This copy of **The Union Jack** is dated 14 January 1897, the Grand Double Number of **Pluck** (at double the usual price) 9 December 1899.

The Boys' Friend. London: Harmsworth Bros./Amalgamated Press. Ed. by Robert Hamilton Edwards/Herbert Allan Hinton/Reginald Thompson Eves.
1st series: 332 issues; 29 January 1895 to 8 June 1901.
2nd series: 1,385 issues; 15 June 1901 to 31 December 1927.

The Boys' Herald, A Healthy Paper for Manly Boys. London: Amalgamated Press. Ed. by Robert Hamilton Edwards/H. A. Hinton. 462 issues.
1 August 1903 to 18 May 1912

The Boys' Realm, A Popular Paper for all British Boys and Young Men. London: Amalgamated Press. Ed. by R. H. Edwards/H. A. Hinton.
1st series as **The Boys' Realm;** 721 issues; 14 June 1902 to 25 March 1916.
2nd series as **The Boys' Realm;** 432 issues; 5 April 1919 to 16 July 1927.
3rd series as **The Boys' Realm of Sport and Adventure;** 82 issues; 23 July 1927 to 9 February 1929.
4th series as **The Boys' Realm of Fun and Fiction;** 51 issues; 16 February 1929 to 1 February 1930.

The Marvel (running title **The "Halfpenny Marvel" Library,** then **The Marvel Library**). London: Harmsworth Brothers/Amalgamated Press. Ed. by Alfred Edgar/Harold Garrish/S. J. Summers/Horace Phillips.
1st series: 533 issues; 11 November 1893 to 23 January 1904.
2nd series: 952 issues; 30 January 1904 to 22 April 1922.

Pluck (running title **The "Pluck" Library**), A High-Class Weekly Library of Adventure at Home and Abroad, on Land and Sea: Being the Daring Deeds of Plucky Sailors, Plucky Soldiers, Plucky Firemen, Plucky Explorers, Plucky Detectives, Plucky Railwaymen, Plucky Boys, Plucky Girls and All Sorts and Conditions of British Heroes. London: Harmsworth Brothers/Amalgamated Press. Ed. by Alfred Edgar/Harold Garrish/Horace Phillips/S. J. Summers.
1st series: 519 issues; 24 November 1894 to 5 November 1904.
2nd series: 594 issues; 12 November 1904 to 25 March 1916.
3rd series: 103 issues; 28 October 1922 to 11 October 1924.

The Union Jack (running title **The "Union Jack" Library**), Library of High-Class Fiction. London: Harmsworth Bros./Amalgamated Press. Ed. by W. H. Maas/S. J. Summers/William Back/Lewis Carlton/Robert Murray Graydon/Walter Shute/H. W. Twyman.
1st series: 494 issues; 28 April 1894 to 10 October 1903.
2nd series: 1,531 issues; 17 October 1903 to 18 February 1933.

The inadequacy of Britain's defences against the German military build-up was heavily underlined in Harmsworth's newspapers and boys' magazines. **The Boy's Friend** of 12 June 1909.

A SPECIAL MESSAGE FROM YOUR EDITOR THIS WEEK. *(See Page 20.)*

THE BOYS' FRIEND 1d,

EVERY TUESDAY.

The object of THE BOYS' FRIEND is to Amuse, to Instruct, and to Advise Boys.

No. 418.—Vol. IX. New Series]   **ONE PENNY.**   [Week Ending June 12, 1909.

The Peril to Come!

A Fleet of Foreign Zeppelin Airships Hovers Over London! *(See Our Grand New Serial Inside.)*

BILLY BUNTER AND SEXTON BLAKE

In the autumn of 1939 George Orwell collected a few dozen copies of boys' weeklies and examined their contents. He came to the conclusion that they preserved the worst illusions of the Edwardian age, presenting a world in which 'the clock has stopped at 1910 and Britannia rules the waves.'[1]

The two magazines he singled out as representative were both published by Amalgamated Press (as the Harmsworth firm had been renamed in 1902): **Gem** (1907) and its companion paper **Magnet** (1908). Orwell could scarcely believe that despite repetitive style and predictable plots, one man had written virtually all the stories in these boys' papers. In his lifetime, Charles Hamilton (1876-1961) composed more than 5,000 stories under 26 pseudonyms; the **Guinness Book of Records** once computed that he had written about 72 million words during his writing career. As Frank Richards, he wrote tales about Greyfriars School for the **Magnet**; and as Martin Clifford, he wrote about St. Jim's for the **Gem** – school stories in which the clock had stopped at 1910.

Working-class boys may never have actually seen a public school in their lives, but they responded warmly to Hamilton's stories. In his autobiography Robert Roberts recalled the way boys used to imitate the language, behaviour and affectations of the characters in the **Gem** and **Magnet** stories. In their enthusiasm, boys from working-class families in Salford used to dash to the railway station to catch the bulk arrival from London and buy the first copies from the bookstall.

Over the years these simple tales conditioned the thought of a whole generation of boys. The public school ethos, distorted into myth and sold among us weekly in penny numbers, for good or ill, set ideals and standards. This our own tutors, religious and secular, had signally failed to do. In the final estimate it may well be found that Frank Richards during the first quarter of the twentieth century had more influence on the mind and outlook of young working-class England than any other single person.[2]

Hamilton created groups of boys in his school stories, boys of varying ages and social backgrounds, each assigned a particular role. Young readers found characters in these stories whose main traits were known to them, boys they could understand and identify with. There was one exception, however, a figure no-one could identify with, a lazy, greedy, pusillanimous, obese schoolboy, forever scrounging a few bob against a postal order that never arrived. He was repeatedly booted down a flight of stairs by the Famous Five whereupon he would utter his inimitable cry of pain, 'Yaroooooh!' Billy Bunter, the Fat Owl of the Remove, was launched in the **Magnet** in 1908 and kept that paper ahead of its companion **Gem** in

[1]George Orwell, 'Boys' Weeklies', in **Horizon**, March 1940 (reprinted in the Penguin edition of his articles and letters).
[2]Robert Roberts, **The Classic Slum**, London, 1971.

G

The School Friend
Every 2d Thursday
No. 270. Vol. 11. Week Ending July 12th, 1924.

circulation until it was discontinued in 1940 because of the paper shortage.[3]

Billy Bunter had a sister, Elizabeth Gertrude Bunter, known as Bessie Bunter (sometimes as Fatima), in rotundity and craftiness a match for her elder brother, but in popularity lagging far behind.[4] Charles Hamilton wrote the first of the girls' school stories for **School Friend** under the pen-name Hilda Richards; the later stories were taken over by Horace Phillips, then John Wheway. (It was characteristic of the girls' papers that they were edited, written and illustrated by men.) Bessie Bunter never really caught on, and A.P. instructed their boys' writers to try their hands at adventure stories for girls, the results of their endeavours filling the pages of the **School Friend** (1919), **Schoolgirls' Weekly** (1922), **Schoolgirl** (1929) and **The Crystal** (1935). The twenties and thirties have been described as the heyday of girls' fiction, a time when girls drove fast cars, chasing spies and jewel-thieves and smashing smugglers' rings; it was the age of the resourceful, high-spirited heroine.[5]

There was yet another strain of popular fiction A.P. cultivated between the wars: detective stories. The first of 4,000 stories by some 200 authors about the detective Sexton Blake, 'the office-boy's Sherlock Holmes', appeared in the **Halfpenny Marvel** in 1893. He was then transferred to the second series of the **Union Jack**, a periodical he eventually dominated to the extent that it was renamed **The Detective Weekly** (1933). Sexton Blake had his own 'library' (this is a small-format magazine published on an irregular basis), as had Nelson Lee, a criminologist who had solved his first case in the **Halfpenny Marvel** in 1894, although he never really attained Sexton Blake's legendary status. A further story-paper **The Thriller** (1929) included mysteries by Edgar Wallace, Toff stories by John Creasey and Saint stories by Leslie Charteris. With all these magazines for boys, girls and young adults, A.P. dominated popular fiction in the inter-war period; but their supremacy was soon to be challenged, not from Fleet Street, London, but from Meadowside, Dundee.

The Champion. London: Amalgamated Press. Ed. by R. T. Eves. 1,729 issues. 28 January 1922 to 19 March 1955. Pre-war circulation around 150,000 copies.

The Detective Weekly, Starring Sexton Blake. London: Amalgamated Press. 379 issues. 25 February 1933 to 25 May 1940.

The Gem (originally **The Gem Library**). London: Amalgamated Press. Principal editors: Percy Griffith/ Herbert Allan Hinton/John Nix Pentelow/C. M. Down. 1st series: 48 issues; 16 March 1907 to 8 February 1908. 2nd series: 1,663 issues; 15 February 1908 to

30 December 1939. Peak circulation some 200,000 copies p.w.; down to 16,000 copies by 1939.

Girls' Cinema. London: Amalgamated Press. 631 issues. 16 October 1920 to 19 November 1932.

The Magnet (originally **The Magnet Library**). London: Amalgamated Press. Ed. by Percy Griffith/H. A. Hinton/ John Nix Pentelow/C. Maurice Down. 1,683 issues. 15 February 1908 to 18 May 1940. Selling in excess of 200,000 copies around 1925-35, but down to 40,000 copies in 1940.

[3]Bunter appeared in a strip in **Knockout** from 1939 to 1962, in **Comet** in 1962 and more recently in **Valiant**. His adventures have appeared in books issued by Skilton, Cassell, Hamlyn (paperbacks), Howard Baker (facsimile editions) and in 1982 a new series re-written by Kay King began, published by Quiller Press. He had his own series on BBC Television in 1952, produced by Joy Harrington.

[4]Bessie Bunter also appeared in **June**, and until quite recently in **Tammy**.

[5]See Mary Cadogan and Patricia Craig, **You're a Brick, Angela!**, London, 1976, chapters 13 and 14.

The Nelson Lee Library. London: Amalgamated Press. Ed. by Harold May (1915-28)/Alfred Edgar (1928-30)/ Jimmy Cauldwell (1930-33).
1st series: 568 issues; 12 June 1915 to 24 April 1926.
2nd series: 194 issues; 1 May 1926 to 18 January 1930.
3rd series: 161 issues; 25 January 1930 to 18 February 1933.
4th series: 25 issues; 25 February to 12 August 1933.

The Penny Popular. London: Amalgamated Press. Ed. by C. M. Down.
1st series: 286 issues; 12 October 1912 to 30 March 1918.
2nd series: 628 issues; 25 January 1919 to 7 February 1931.

The Ranger. London: Amalgamated Press. 130 issues. 14 February 1931 to 5 August 1933.

The School Friend. London: Amalgamated Press. Ed. by Reginald Eves.
1st series: 303 issues; 17 May 1919 to 28 February 1925.

2nd series: 229 issues; 7 March 1925 to 27 July 1929. Continued under the title **Schoolgirl,** 1929-40.

The Sexton Blake Library. London: Amalgamated Press/ Mayflower Books. Ed. by W. Home-Gall (1915-19)/Len Pratt (1920-55)/W. Howard Baker (1956-70).
1st series: 382 numbers; 20 September 1915 to 4 May 1925.
2nd series: 744 numbers; 3 June 1925 to October 1940.
3rd series: 358 numbers; November 1940 to May 1956.
4th series: 168 numbers; June 1956 to June 1963.
5th series: 49 numbers; February 1965 to 1970.

The Thriller, The Paper with a Thousand Thrills. London: Amalgamated Press. Ed. by Leonard E. Pratt. 589 numbers. 9 February 1929 to 18 May 1940.

The Triumph. London: Amalgamated Press. Ed. by R. T. Eves. 814 numbers. 18 October 1924 to 25 May 1940.

The Union Jack, see under section F.

Magnet, 12 June 1937.

Gem, 9 July 1927.

For all his criticism of the ethos of Greyfriars, even George Orwell had to admit that Billy Bunter was 'a really first-rate character and one of the best-known figures in English fiction'.

The Sexton Blake Library dated 2 March 1928.

Girls' Cinema consisted of stories woven round film stills. (This issue is dated 30 October 1930.)

Charles Hamilton wrote school stories for **The School Friend** under the pen-name 'Hilda Richards'. (This number is dated 12 July 1924.)

THE BIG FIVE

The A.P. monopoly of the juvenile market was finally broken by a Scottish firm, D.C. Thomson & Co. of Dundee, founded in 1905 in order to consolidate the printing and publishing interests acquired more or less by accident by a family with considerable shipping interests. It was evident from the start that shrewd market-analysis preceded their new publishing ventures, papers and magazines providing light reading for working-class readers. **My Weekly** was turned into a highly successful women's magazine, and even more popular was their **Sunday Post** (1920) which today is read by around 80% of the adult population of Scotland. Nothing succeeds like success, and by the early eighties the firm was publishing and printing more than 12 million copies of their papers and comics per week and more than a million magazines a month![1]

In the 1920s the Thomsons turned their attention to boys' papers. They apparently realized that a diet of school-japes and soft-boiled sleuth-stories was palatable to working-class boys only so long as nothing else was offered them. R.D. Low, managing editor of the Big Five, as the clutch of new story-papers came to be known, showed a clear grasp of the basic principle that the boys' thriller had to be thrilling. **Adventure** appeared in 1921, followed by **Rover** and **Wizard** in 1922, the **Skipper** in 1930 and **Hotspur** in 1933.[2] The title of the first of these story-papers announced a return to adventure, hard, fast, and tough, adventure of a traditional kind in stories about the perils of the jungle, wars in the colonies, the world of sport and school. But side by side with this were the really innovative stories, incorporating strong elements of fantasy and magic. The new heroes were supermen (Morgyn the Mighty), outrageous animals (O'Neill, the Six-Gun Gorilla), good-natured robots (The Iron Teacher) and strange prodigies (the Incredible Wilson, born in 1795, whose longevity and virility were ascribed to his diet of grass and wild berries and who periodically emerged from his cave in the Pennines to break the latest world record in long-distance running). 'Plausibility and probability never worried the writers from beyond the Tweed', E.S. Turner writes, 'their chief concern seems to have been to avoid any charge of conventionality'.[3]

What Thomson, boys, parents, and newsagents must have known for some time was confirmed in a study of children's preferred reading published in 1940: the Big Five, those 'monstrously successful "bloods"' as **The Times Literary Supplement** called them, topped the popularity polls by a wide margin.[4] One of the five was killed off by paper-shortage after Germany invaded Norway in 1940, but despite the war, and the appeal of the new comics **Beano** and **Dandy** (also from the

[1]See George Rosie et al., **The D.C. Thomson Bumper Fun Book**, Edinburgh, 1977.
[2]A.P. took up the challenge and issued a series of similar boys' papers: **Champion** (1922), **Rocket** (1923), **Triumph** (1924), **Modern Boy** (1928), **Bullseye** (1931) and **The Ranger** (1931).
[3]E.S. Turner, **Boys Will Be Boys**, Penguin, 1976 (1948).
[4]A.J. Jenkinson's book **What Do Boys and Girls Read?** was reviewed in **The Times Literary Supplement** on 1 June 1940.

H

Thomson stable), and competition from TV after the war, the other four survived. In the end, the inexorable progress of the strip caught up with them, and in 1959 the **Hotspur** was transformed overnight into a picture-paper, its closely printed text and line illustrations becoming picture sequences with speech balloons. The last of the old-style story-papers, the **Rover**, soldiered on until it finally collapsed in 1973. The boys' adventure picture-paper had finally won the day.

Conventional weapons are no match for the versatility of the Snatcher. **The Skipper** of 24 December 1938.

Adventure. London: D. C. Thomson. Ed. by R. D. Low. 1,878 issues. 17 September 1921 to 14 January 1961.

The Hotspur (story-paper). London: D. C. Thomson. Ed. by W. Blain/R. D. Low. 1,197 issues. 2 September 1933 to 17 October 1959.

Hotspur (picture-paper). London: D. C. Thomson. 1st series as **The New Hotspur;** 173 issues; 24 October 1959 to 9 February 1963.
2nd series as **Hotspur;** commenced 16 February 1963 and still running.

The Rover. London: D. C. Thomson. Ed. by R. D. Low.
1st series: 1,855 issues; 4 March 1922 to 14 January 1961.
2nd series: approx. 630 issues; 21 January 1961 to 13 January 1973.

The Skipper. London: D. C. Thomson. Ed. by A. Hunter 543 issues. 6 September 1930 to 1 February 1941.

The Wizard (story-paper). London: D. C. Thomson. Ed. by W. D. Blain. 1,970 issues. 23 September 1922 to 16 November 1963. Pre-war peak circulation 800,000 copies p.w.

Wizard (picture-paper). London: D. C. Thomson. 435 issues. 14 February 1970 to 24 June 1978.
Began at 500,000 copies p.w., finally down to 130,000.

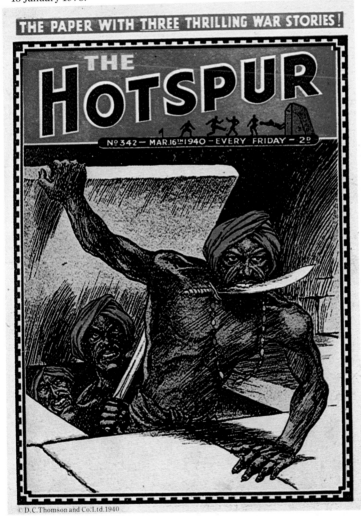

© D. C. Thomson and Co. Ltd. 1940

The Indian Mutiny story in this issue of **The Hotspur** (dated 16 March 1940) re-appeared as an adventure strip in the **New Hotspur** in 1966.

SOME FORERUNNERS OF THE COMIC

The comic strip, defined as a narrative in the form of a sequence of pictures with or without text, can boast a respectable ancestry according to **The Penguin Book of Comics**, which traces its genealogy back to palaeolithic cave paintings, Mexican codices, and the Bayeux tapestry.[1] Balloonless strips are found on European broadsheets, particularly on German *Bilderbogen*, which dealt primarily with political and religious themes, but also encompassed stories and fairy-tales.[2] Captions, speech-balloons, and drawn-in panel borders were not invented by the artists working for the comics; they were employed regularly by the English caricaturists of the late eighteenth century. In many ways these caricatures anticipate techniques usually associated with modern comics: techniques of condensation, highlighting, and characterization through facial expression or body posture.[3] Hogarth's work and the **Beano** are of course worlds apart in artistic complexity and didactic function, and it would not be easy to argue that there is a direct line of descent between the two. The simple definition of the comic strip in the first sentence of this paragraph will obviously not take us very far; other elements and developments have to be taken into account. One critical difference, for example, is the audience. At a shilling a piece the old caricatures could only reach a small, well-to-do clientele; an essential component in any definition of the comic strip is that it is a mass medium, produced for, read and enjoyed by millions of ordinary people. This presupposes widespread literacy and interest in entertaining literature, and also cheap methods of producing such a literature in quantity.

The caricatures had been etched on copper plates which could only sustain a print of a few hundred copies. Text and picture could not easily be combined until the practice of engraving original drawings on very durable boxwood blocks had been adopted. These blocks could be printed along with metal type, and could be used many times over; that is, illustrated matter could now be printed quickly, cheaply, and in vast quantities. William Hone's political pamphlet **The Political House that Jack Built**, 1819, with illustrations by Cruikshank, went through some 50 editions, and marked the beginning of the relatively uncomplicated combination of word and image in printed form. Within a few years, illustrated newspapers, novels, magazines, and children's books were the order of the day. A balance between text and illustration was not always easy to achieve, and there were some notable excesses: Samuel Beeton's edition of **Don Quixote** boasted nearly 700 illustrations on 766 pages of print.

Once newspaper taxes had been reduced, faster and cheaper presses set up, and efficient distribution services established, the newspaper press expanded at a rapid rate. Some saw the 'penny press' as a bad thing for the people, a force

I

[1]George Perry and Alan Aldridge, **The Penguin Book of Comics**, 1967.
[2]David Kunzle, **The Early Comic Strip**, Berkeley & Los Angeles, 1973.
[3]See 'Caricature, Cartoon, and Comic Strip' in **Encyclopaedia Britannica**.

undermining established order in society. Even the new illustrated papers for more respectable circles came in for criticism; papers such as **The Illustrated London News** (1842) and **The Pictorial Times** (1843) were not universally welcomed. William Wordsworth recorded his disgust in a poem:

> A backward movement surely we have here,
> From manhood – back to childhood; for the age –
> Back towards caverned life's first rude career.
> Avaunt this vile abuse of pictured page!
> Must eyes be all in all, the tongue and ear
> Nothing? Heaven keep us from a lower stage![4]

But for all the criticism, there were far more newspaper purchasers who must have found that the wood engravings, whether depicting a Chartist demonstration or a state visit, added immediacy to news reports. These illustrations were so successful that by mid-century a new occupation had emerged: staff artist to a newspaper. **The Graphic** even evolved a style of presenting events in a page of 7 to 10 pictures – the latest news in comic-strip form.

There was room in the weeklies for humorous comic strips as well. On display is a volume of **The Graphic** of 1888 which contains a colour-printed strip by A. Marie called **English Officers Abroad – Fox-Hunting in Egypt**. It is difficult to grasp this strip quickly as the pictures are not presented in a logical sequence. The best-known of the humorous strips to appear in the illustrated weeklies is probably **The Adventures of Mr. Verdant Green, An Oxford Freshman** by Cuthbert Bede B.A. (pen-name of Rev. Edward Bradley), printed in **The Illustrated London News** in 1852 and expanded into 3 volumes in 1854-57.

Of all the humorous magazines of the Victorian age, **Punch** (1841) alone has survived up to the present day. During his time on the **Punch** staff, from 1841 to 1850, Richard Doyle contributed numerous short strips, including a series about the travels of three companions, whose adventures in Europe appeared in book-form in 1854 under the title **The Foreign Tour of Messrs. Brown, Jones & Robinson**. In its political caricatures, **Punch** returned to the style of the late eighteenth century, establishing the full-page political cartoon, the forerunner of today's editorial cartoon. One of these early topical cartoons, John Leech's famous **The Home of the Rick-Burner** (1844), expressing sympathy with the starving country workers of Suffolk, captures well the critical, radical tone of the early **Punch.** Before long, however, **Punch** had modified its policies, becoming a magazine for the upper-middle classes and articulating their view of the world. Among the offspring of **Punch** were **Fun** (1861), **Judy** (1867) and **Funny Folks** (1874), all of which set their sights on a working-class and lower-middle-class readership; the comic paper had begun to reach out to a mass audience.

[4]Lines from **Illustrated Books and Newspapers**, written in 1846 and published in 1850.

On the continent, the artists working for Kaspar Braun's **Fliegende Blätter** (1844) had been presenting humorous situations and incidents in a series of pictures for some time. The most proficient amongst these artists was Wilhelm Busch, whose picture stories anticipated the comics in economy of drawing style, situational comedy, the stylized expression of emotion, and even the use of 'speed lines'. Busch's most enduring creation was that prank-loving pair Max and Moritz, whose practical jokes – they were the first comic-strip schoolboys to blow up their teacher – appeared in 1865. The American newspaper magnate W. R. Hearst saw a copy during a visit to Europe in 1896 and commissioned Rudolph Dirks to produce something along similar lines, the result being the Katzenjammer Kids (1897), who themselves begat dozens of 'terrible twins' strips in English comics.[5] The picture story by Busch that appeared in the Christmas number of **The Young Briton** in 1869 was doubtless reprinted without his knowledge, as were the strips printed in E. J. Brett's **Boys of England** and **Young Men of Great Britain** between 1872 and 1877 and **Our Boys' Journal** between 1876 and 1878.[6]

The first comic strip in an English children's periodical appeared between 4 September and 13 November 1868 in the **Boys of England;** it portrayed the rivalry between two figures, Long and Short, on a page of nine vertically arranged panels. In 1883 E. J. Brett came very close to publishing the first comic created for young people. His **Boy's Comic Journal** contained two and a half pages of cartoons and strips from American and continental sources, including the regular feature **Sam Sly's Comic Picture Gallery**. Despite its title, however, **The Boy's Comic Journal** was basically a story-paper, the adventure serial remaining the key ingredient. Children had to wait until the early twentieth century for the first comic specifically designed for their entertainment.

This section contains volumes of **Punch, The Illustrated London News, The Graphic** and Brett's boys' papers **Boys of England, Young Men of Great Britain** and **The Boy's Comic Journal** (for details of these three story-papers see under section A). The broadsheet **Ein Neujahrsconzert**, kindly lent by the Wilhelm Busch Museum in Hanover, appeared as a supplement in vol. 43 of the **Fliegende Blätter** in 1865; it is better known in Germany as **Der Virtuos**, the title under which it was re-issued in the **Münchener Bilderbogen** in 1868. Two issues of **Funny**

[5]Busch's work was also brought out by better-known publishing houses (Griffith & Farran; John Camden Hotten; A. N. Myers), some of it with excellent colour reproduction.

[6]Max and Moritz appeared as Tootle and Bootle in **Comic Cuts** in 1896. Dirks's Katzenjammer Kids ran in **Big Budget** in 1902 and in **Comic Life** in 1910. Derivative strips include: The Boys (1896) in **Comic Cuts**; Those Terrible Twins in **The Halfpenny Comic** in 1898 and in **Larks!** in 1902; Our Kids (1898) in **Comic Cuts**; The Twinkleton Twins (1899) in **The Big Budget**; The Bunsey Boys (1902) in **Jester and Wonder**; Fritz and Jakey (1909) in **Comic Life**; Willie and Wally (1914) in **The Funny Wonder**; Tim and Tom (1914) in **The Big Comic**; and, above all, The Terrible Twins in **Comic Cuts** from 1918 to 1937.

Folks, recently declared the first British comic,[7] are included here to demonstrate trends leading to the comics boom of the 1890s (details of **Funny Folks** will be found under Section J).

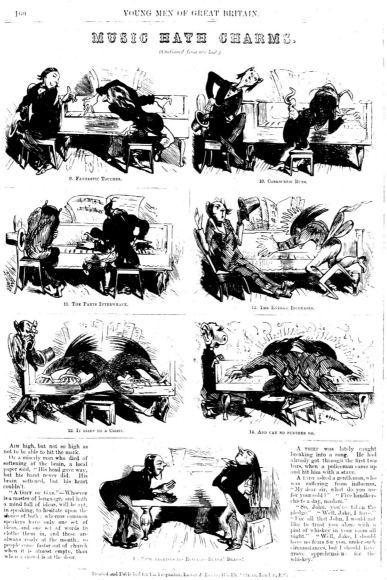

It is unlikely that Wilhelm Busch ever knew that his satirical picture-story **Der Virtuos** was translated and re-engraved in London for E. J. Brett. From the back page of **Young Men of Great Britain** dated 9 September 1872.

[7]Denis Gifford, **The British Comic Catalogue 1874 to 1974**, London, 1975.

American support for the Fenians, the physical force wing
of the Irish Land League, is lampooned in this political
cartoon by Stafford in **Funny Folks** of 22 April 1882.

No. 386—Vol. VIII.]   For the Week Ending Saturday, April 22, 1882.   [Registered at the General Post Office as a Newspaper.
[Price ONE PENNY. By Post, 1½d.

FUNNY FOLKS

THE COMIC COMPANION TO THE NEWSPAPER.

"Our True Intent is all for your Delight."—*Shakespeare.*

THE ATTITUDE OF AMERICA.

EARLY ENGLISH COMICS

Ally Sloper's Half-Holiday (1884), published by the Dalziel brothers, established the layout of the British comic. Its centre and back pages were crammed with cartoons and short strips, and on page one it featured the first regular character in the comics. Ally Sloper F.O.M. (Friend of Man) had first seen printer's ink in the pages of **Judy** in 1867, and his adventures were collected into the first comic book in 1873, **Ally Sloper: A Moral Lesson**. Ally Sloper–his name is a pun on the practice of dodging the rent collector by sloping down the alley–was the creation of Charles Ross and his wife Marie Duval; the figure was later taken over by the American-born artist W. G. Baxter, and then by W. F. Thomas. Whether selling rotten oysters on Brighton beach, duelling with Boulanger, enlightening magistrates on a point of law, or holding forth on the Freedom of the Individual whilst snuffing a heckler like a farthing dip, Ally always came out on top; it helped, of course, that those he duped were conceited numbskulls who deserved humiliation at his hands. The embodiment of cheerful insolence and unabashed self-interest, Ally Sloper was the first in a long line of rogues as heroes in the comics, which extends to today's Andy Capp.

The comics boom actually began wsith **Comic Cuts** (1890). This paper was put together in three weeks at the instigation of Alfred Harmsworth to publicize and boost the flagging sales of his **Answers** (1888), which had been his scissors-and-paste reply to George Newnes's scissors-and-paste **Tit-Bits. Comic Cuts** itself was a kind of illustrated **Answers**, made up of odds and ends mainly lifted from American humourous papers. However, it soon carried a line in thick type requesting 'clever artists' to submit their work, and within a year most of the material was original. The fragmented layout of **Comic Cuts** coupled with its visual impact evidently appealed to the Board School educated young adults Harmsworth regarded as his clients. The price, a halfpenny, was a rock-bottom price for a cheap paper, and many newsagents refused to handle the comic protesting that their profit margin was too slight. Harmsworth used to say that for every man prepared to spend a shilling on a magazine, there were thousands prepared to risk a halfpenny, and sales of his papers proved him right. The Harmsworthian 'halfpenny principle' was based on an exact analysis of the potential market, an assessment of the state of the printing trade (stagnant wages, cheaper paper, improved machinery), and an awareness that there was an army of writers and illustrators in London looking for work.[1]

Comic Cuts's first edition of 120,000 copies was sold within hours and within weeks its circulation had risen to 300,000 copies. By early 1892 Harmsworth could boast of a readership of two and a half million, with a scornful reminder that most of the forty or fifty imitations has 'died a lingering death.'[2] Some of these imitations did,

J

[1] See Alan J. Lee, **The Origins of the Popular Press in England, 1855-1914,** London, 1976.
[2] 'How the Greatest Comic Paper in the World is Produced,' in **Comic Cuts** dated 2 February 1892.

however, survive for many years, among them **Funny Cuts** (1890) and **Snap-Shots** (1890), despite further competition from Harmsworth's own **Illustrated Chips** (1890), **Funny Wonder** (1892) and the **Comic Home Journal** (1895). By 1891 the colloquialism 'comic' had become common usage.[3]

Features of today's comics, such as the full-page strip, speech balloons, regular characters, and colour printing, were all established in the late nineteenth century. The single-picture cartoons in the early comics developed into two, then three panels to present a before/after gag, the change in a situation, person or object (an 'evolution'), or to illustrate a sequence of related events. These strips took over more and more space, until **Comic Cuts** had its first full-page comic strip on 14 February 1891, **Illustrated Chips** following suit a few weeks later on 4 April. Speech stayed in the captions until comparatively late; in 1900 it began to hover in longhand near the figures. It was Ralph Hodgson ('Yorick') who began to use the speech balloon systematically and sensibly in 1901. Alfred Gray had produced asymmetrical borderless panels in the early 1890s, but the drawn-in panel border had become conventional by the late nineties. Regular use of colour came with the **Coloured Comic** in 1898, but it did not mix well with the cramped page dotted with blacked areas. **Comic Life**, printed in colour from 1909, showed how colour could be properly integrated as a component in a comic strip.

The cartoons in the early comics caricatured supposed types: the fashion addict; the policeman; the cook; the tramp; the mother-in-law; the 'spooner'; the 'masher'. **Comic Life** was the odd man out amongst the comics in that up to around 1904 its humour was often topical and political, and its barbs were not infrequently directed against politicians, socialists and New Women.

As the strips began to supplant the cartoons, it was realized that readers became attached to their favourite figures, who settled down in their own corner of a particular page. The first regular characters to emerge in the 1890s comics were two amiable tramps, Weary Willie and Tired Tim, created in 1896 by Tom Browne and based on two down-and-outs he had spotted on Thames Embankment. Browne invented a second set of tramps he called Airy Alf and Bouncing Billy for **Big Budget** in 1897 (the strip was taken over by Hodgson in 1899). Browne also produced Little Willy and Tiny Tim for **Chips's** younger readers. Although comics at this time were still produced for the young adult, publishers calculated on having children among their readers. Henderson had declared of his **Funny Folks** that 'children will grow merry with it, and even baby will laugh and crow over the picture pages', and **Chips** had described itself as 'The "Kid" Quietener, Father's Comfort, and Mother's Joy.'

[3]'There are many so-called "comics," but only one **Comic Cuts**' (**Illustrated Chips** dated 10 October 1891).

James Henderson's **Comic Life** was founded in 1898, went coloured in 1909, became a children's comic in 1918, was taken over by Amalgamated Press in 1920, changed its name to **My Favourite** in 1928, and finally disappeared in 1934.

Between the creation of his World-Famous Tramps in 1896 and his departure from comics in 1900, Tom Browne had created the style of the modern British comic.[4] Many artists copied his tidy but bold linework, and absorbed his knack of adapting farcical themes to the exigencies of the six to nine-panel strip. Browne had started his career in comics by doing work for Cassell's **Chums** between 1892 and 1895, along with Jack B. Yeats. Yeats stayed in the business longer, and produced some highly eccentric figures for the early comics; but while there was a definite Browne school, Yeats remained something of a loner.[5] The slapstick, gags and style of modern comics had crystalized by the end of the nineteenth century. The world where violence does not really hurt anybody and where the pompous get their cum-uppance as the little man's ingenuity wins the day, was as familiar to late-Victorian readers as it is to today's children.

[4]Denis Gifford (ed.), **Victorian Comics**, London, 1976.
[5]Among Yeats's odd characters were the detective Chubblock Homes (1894); Ephriam Broadbeamer, the Pimply Nosed Smuggler, Pirate and Other Things (1897); the stubborn horse Signor McCoy (1897); the con-man Hiram B. Boss (1898); and the weird mechanical dog Who-Did-It (1907).

Ally Sloper's Half-Holiday, Being a Selection, Side-Splitting, Sentimental, and Serious, for the Benefit of Old Boys, Young Boys, Odd Boys Generally, and Even Girls. London: W. J. Simkins/Gilbert Dalziel at "The Sloperies"/ Milford. Ed. by Charles Ross/Gilbert Dalziel. 1,570 issues. 3 May 1884 to 30 May 1914.
Peak circulation approx. 350,000 copies p.w. There have been several attempts to revive the name of this popular comic: 1914-16, 1922-23, 1948, 1949 and 1976.

The Big Budget. London: 28, Maiden Lane [i.e. C. Arthur Pearson]. Ed. by Arthur Brooke; art editor 'Yorick' [i.e. Ralph Hodgson]. 614 issues. 19 June 1897 to 20 March 1909.

The Big Comic. London: James Henderson & Sons. 207 issues. 17 January 1914 to 29 December 1917.

The Coloured Comic. London: Trapps, Holmes & Co. 415 issues. 21 May 1898 to 28 April 1906.
The first English comic printed in colour.

Comic Cuts, One Hundred Laughs for a Halfpenny. London: Answers Company/Pandora Publishing Company/ Amalgamated Press. Ed. by G. H. Cantle/R. N. Chance. 3,006 issues. 17 May 1890 to 12 September 1953.
By 1892 430,000 copies p.w.; prior to World War I up to approx. 1 million copies.

The Comic Home Journal. London: Carmelite House [i.e. Harmsworth Brothers]/Amalgamated Press. Ed. by G. H. Cantle. 488 issues. 11 May 1895 to 10 September 1904.
A continuation of the short-lived **Boys' Home Journal.**

Comic Life, The Amusing Picture-Paper for the People. Original title **Pictorial Comic-Life.** London: James Henderson & Sons/Amalgamated Press. 1,543 issues. 14 May 1898 to 21 January 1928.

The Favorite Comic. London: Amalgamated Press. Ed. by Fred Cordwell. 324 issues. 21 January 1911 to 31 March 1917.

Funny Cuts. London: Trapps, Holmes & Co. Ed. by Gordon Phillip Hood. 1,566 issues. 12 July 1890 to 3 July 1920.
With **The World's Comic** sold 600,000 copies p.w. in 1892.

Funny Folks, A Weekly Budget of Funny Pictures – Funny Notes – Funny Jokes – Funny Stories. London: James Henderson. 1,614 issues. 12 December 1874 to 28 April 1894.
The first British comic.

Funny Pips. London: 28, Maiden Lane [i.e. C. Arthur Pearson]. Ed. by Arthur Brooke. 16 issues. 12 September to 26 December 1903.
Free supplement with the story-paper **The Boys' Leader.**

The Funny Wonder, see **The Wonder.**

Illustrated Chips. London: Harmsworth Brothers/B. W. Young/Pandora Press/Amalgamated Press. Ed. by G. H. Cantle/R. N. Chance.
1st series: 6 issues; 26 July 1890 to 30 August 1890.
2nd series: 2,997 issues. 6 September 1890 to 12 September 1953.
At the height of its popularity was selling 1 million copies a week.

Larks! London: Gilbert Dalziel/Trapps, Holmes & Co.
1st series: 462 issues; 1 May 1893 to 3 March 1902.
2nd series: 239 issues; 7 June 1902 to 29 December 1906.

Lot-o'-Fun. London: James Henderson/Amalgamated Press. Ed. by Alfred Barrett. 1,196 issues. 17 March 1906 to 16 February 1929.

Pictorial Comic-Life, see **Comic Life.**

Puck, Jokes and Pictures for the Home. London: Carmelite House/Fleetway House/Amalgamated Press. 1,867 issues. 30 July 1904 to 11 May 1940.

Snap-Shots, Humorous Pictures and Amusing Reading Chiefly from Advance Proofs of Current American Papers by Exclusive Arrangement. London: James Henderson. Approx. 1,030 issues. 9 August 1890 to 30 April 1910.

The Wonder. London: 24, Tudor Street [i.e. Harmsworth Brothers]/Amalgamated Press. Ed. G. H. Cantle/Harry Garrish/Stanley Gooch.
1st series as **The Wonder;** 27 issues; 30 July 1892 to 27 January 1893.
2nd series as **The Funny Wonder;** 325 issues; 4 February 1893 to 22 April 1899.
3rd series as **The Funny Wonder;** 109 issues; 29 April 1899 to 25 May 1901.
4th series as **The Wonder;** 24 issues; 1 June 1901 to 9 November 1901.
5th series as **The Wonder;** 25 issues; 16 November 1901 to 3 May 1902.
6th series as **The Wonder and Jester;** 2 issues; 10 May to 17 May 1902.
7th series as **The Jester and Wonder;** 506 issues; 24 May 1902 to 20 January 1912 (continued as **The Jester**).
8th series as **The Penny Wonder;** 47 issues; 10 February 1912 to 28 December 1912.
9th series as **The Wonder;** 64 issues; 4 January 1913 to 21 March 1914.
10th series as **The Halfpenny Wonder;** 39 issues; 28 March 1914 to 19 December 1914.
11th series as **The Funny Wonder;** 1,404 issues; 26 December 1914 to 16 May 1942.
12th series as **The Wonder;** 317 issues; 30 May 1942 to 12 September 1953.

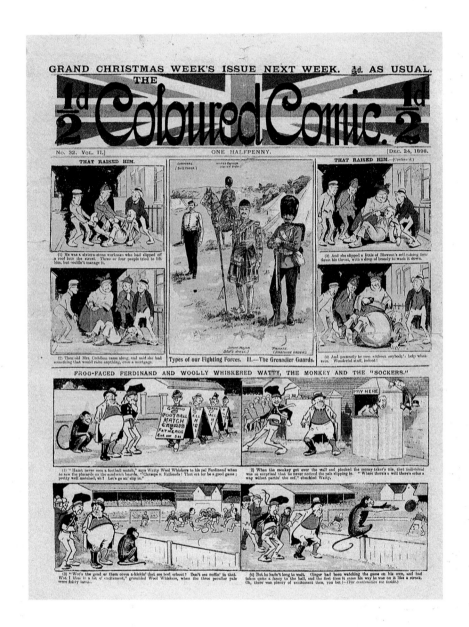

The Coloured Comic, a halfpenny comic issued by Trapps,
Holmes & Co. The above number is dated
24 December 1898.

The Irish artist Jack B. Yeats drew Chubblock Homes for **The Funny Wonder** (above issue dated 10 April 1897).

Bertie Brown specialised in drawing film stars. From **The Funny Wonder,** 13 January 1917.

A suffragette takes to her heels as Wearie Willie and Tired Tim career through the streets in the runabout they have 'borrowed'. From **Illustrated Chips,** 1 August 1908.

Ally Sloper and freedom of speech. From **Ally Sloper's Half-Holiday** dated 20 January 1906.

CHILDREN'S COMICS BETWEEN THE WARS

The **Boy's Comic Journal** (1883) was the first English children's periodical to incorporate cartoons and humorous strips from American and continental sources, although the adventure serial still remained the predominant element. If a comic has to include a number of strips to qualify as a comic, then **Jack and Jill** (1885), which was made up of humorous material, cartoons, anecdotes, but did not include picture stories of any kind, can only be classified as a humorous paper. It would seem that the first comic devised for children was **Funny Pips** which appeared for 16 weeks as a supplement to C. Arthur Pearson's **Boys' Leader** in 1903; the attractive front-page strip **Sunny Jim and Dismal David** was signed by 'Yorick' (i.e. Ralph Hodgson).

Publishers began to cash in on children's interest in comics produced for their parents, elder brothers and sisters. On 8 October 1904 **Puck** brought out a supplement **Junior Puck,** which was soon to take over the whole paper. The first coloured comic exclusively for a child audience, **Rainbow,** appeared on St. Valentine's Day 1914. In 1918 **Comic Life** featured a boy and girl on the front page, Ted and Tot, who soon pushed the other adult figures into the background as children replaced their parents as readers of Henderson's comic. In similar fashion **Sparks** changed its name and clientele in 1920 to become **Little Sparks.** The twenties and thirties saw further expansion with **Tiger Tim's Weekly** (1920), **The Chicks' Own** (1920), **Sunbeam** (1922), **Playbox** (1925), **Tiny Tots** (1927), **Crackers** (1929) and the first photogravure comics **Mickey Mouse Weekly** (1936) and **Happy Days** (1938).

After the price realignment at Amalgamated Press in late 1922 all these comics cost 2d, whereas the 'black comics' of this era cost a penny each (see section L). The price was partly dictated by expensive colour printing, as the first page was printed in full colour and 3 of the remaining 11 pages in red and black. Since the purchasers of these comics were parents rather than children themselves, they had to be convinced that the papers were respectable, if not educationally useful. The two comics aimed at the nursery age group even purported to be reading aids and for years the words in speech balloons were separated into hyphenated syllables. ('The child-ren felt ver-y ex-cit-ed as they made their way home-ward-s with all the pre-sent-s that nur-sie had bought.')

The milieu of the comic strips was decidedly posh: the home was spacious and well-heated; father had a new car; the children were looked after by nursie or nana. A.P.'s strategy of appealing to a middle-class audience, not traditionally thought of as comics-consumers, certainly paid off. **The Rainbow** ('The Children's Paper Parents Approve Of') reached a weekly circulation of around a million copies, one of which was delivered to Buckingham Palace for the Princesses Elizabeth and Margaret.

There is a genteel, sedate air about **The Rainbow**. The front-page strip about Tiger Tim and his friends is never exciting, and is not even enlivened by the colour contrasts; week after week all ends well in the final panel, the depiction of Order Restored. The highly decorative **Happy Days**, on the other hand, creates an impression of nervous energy. The reader's eye moves zig-zag within the panels, taking in all the hectic motion leading up to the hullabaloo of the last panel. The front covers of **Happy Days** were drawn by Roy Wilson, who perfected what could be called the 'avalanche technique' (snowball would be too mild a metaphor), beginning a strip with a situation which rapidly gets out of control, accelerating through the remaining panels, finally smashing into the bottom of the page and rebounding up the margins.

The humanized animal appeared on the front pages of **The Rainbow, Happy Days** and most of the coloured comics of this era. Tiger Tim, the oldest of these characters and the oldest regular character in English comics, first appeared in **The Daily Mirror** in 1904 before moving over to **The Rainbow**, where he was drawn by Julius Baker and then by Herbert Foxwell. After further spells in **Playhour** and **Playbox**, Tiger Tim finally settled down in 1966 in the pages of **Jack and Jill**, where at the age of 79 he is still going strong. There were many other animal figures: **The Chicks' Own** starred Rupert the Chick, drawn by Arthur White; three of Polly and Pat's 'merry friends' in **Little Sparks** were an elephant, a parrot and a mouse. Besides these animal strips, there were stories, puzzles, games, and an increasing number of picture stories. **Puck** had been presenting children's classics and fairy-tales as early as 1917; **Robinson Crusoe**, for instance, on 24 March of that year. Both **Sparks** and **The Rainbow** had strips about the adventures of destitute little orphans (one of these tots' thrillers is entitled **Lonely Dan; or, I Want To Find My Mummy**), and it was the children's comic, **Puck** which contained the first adventure strip in an English comic, Walter Booth's **Rob the Rover**, commencing on 15 May 1920.

The Chicks' Own. London: Amalgamated Press. Ed. by Langton Townley. 1,605 issues. 25 September 1920 to 9 March 1957.

Chuckles. London: Amalgamated Press. Ed. by Lewis Ross Higgins/Herbert Hinton. 517 issues. 10 January 1914 to 1 December 1923.

Happy Days. London: Amalgamated Press. Ed. by John L. Bott. 45 issues. 8 October 1938 to 5 August 1939. Printed in photogravure.

Mickey Mouse Weekly. London: Willbank Publications/Odhams Press. Ed. by William Levy. 920 issues. 8 February 1936 to 28 December 1957.
The first photogravure comic to appear in Britain.

My Favourite. London: Amalgamated Press. Ed. by Florence Pearce. 351 issues. 28 January 1928 to 13 October 1934.

Playbox. London: Amalgamated Press. Ed. by Bill Fisher. 1,279 issues. 14 February 1925 to 11 June 1955.

Puck, see under section J.

The Rainbow, The Children's Paper That Parents Approve Of. London: Amalgamated Press. Ed. by Bill Fisher. 1,898 issues. 14 February 1914 to 28 April 1956. Peak circulation approx. 1 million copies p.w.

Humanized animals existed in the comics long before the idea was taken up by Walt Disney. **Little Sparks** dated 11 March 1922.

Sparks. London: James Henderson (to 1920)/
Amalgamated Press.
1st series as **Sparks;** 198 issues; 21 March 1914 to
29 December 1917.
2nd series as **The Big Comic and Sparks;** 38 issues;
5 January to 26 April 1919.
3rd series as **Sparks and the Big Comic;** 30 issues;
5 October 1918 to 26 April 1919.
4th series as **Sparks;** 51 issues; 3 May 1919 to
17 April 1920.
5th series as **Little Sparks;** 4 issues; 24 April to
15 May 1920.
6th series as **Little Sparks;** 124 issues; 22 May 1920 to

30 September 1922.

Sunbeam. London: Amalgamated Press.
1st series: 173 issues; 7 October 1922 to 23 January 1926.
2nd series: 747 issues; 30 January 1926 to 25 May 1940.

Tiger Tim's Weekly. London: Amalgamated Press. Ed. by
Bill Fisher.
1st series: 94 issues; 31 January 1920 to 12 November 1921.
2nd series: 965 issues; 19 November 1921 to 18 May 1940.

Tiny Tots, The Little One's Own Paper. London:
Amalgamated Press. Ed. by Langton Townley/Basil
Reynolds. 1,344 issues. 22 October 1927 to 24 January 1959.

PENNY COMICS
OF THE TWENTIES AND THIRTIES

Although most of them were printed on tinted paper, they were often called 'black comics', this group of around a dozen newspaper-format comics produced for lower-middle-class and working-class families: **Larks, Jester, Joker, Butterfly, Favourite Comic, Jolly Comic** and others, including the veterans **Comic Cuts** and **Chips**. Costing a penny a piece from the general price reduction at A.P. in the autumn of 1922 up to the Second World War, they were all much of a muchness, with 4 pages of serialized story in small print and 4 pages of humorous strips. Through these two decades the adventure strip gradually took over the last page, although without displacing the conventional mystery and adventure serials, whilst the humorous strips became more and more crowded, the first-page strip evolving from 9 panels to 12 (it has been 6 panels in the 1890s). The comic figures themselves became more and more rubbery and convulsive in their movements, the background more and more detailed. The centre spread was even more chaotic, with up to 7 horizontal and vertical strips and a sprinkling of cartoons. In 1925 **Chips** came up with a strip called **Chips' Comic Cinema**, which stretched across the bottom of the centre pages; with its tiny, thumbnail panels, it was supposed to resemble a yard of film. The funny pages in these comics were drawn by a team of artists – Roy Wilson, Bertie Brown, George Wakefield, Frank Minnitt, Don Newhouse, Alex Akerbladh, the Parlett brothers – who between them ensured that every panel exuded liveliness as the hilarity reached a new pitch of intensity and the slapstick became wilder and wilder (Bonk! Biff! Ow! Whop!).

The variety of comics available at this time – coloured comics and cheap penny comics – and the quality of their innovative art-work have prompted one comics historian to dub the thirties the 'Golden Age of English Comics'.[1] It was a decade when the monopoly of Amalgamated Press was being challenged by Fleetway Press (soon to be absorbed by A.P.), and firms operating from outside London. Provincial Comics, subsequently known as Target Publications, imitated the layout and style of A.P. material only to discover that such a policy was not commercially viable.[2] Meanwhile, north of the border, a completely new strain of comics was being devised and these papers **The Dandy Comic** (1937), **The Beano Comic** (1938) and **The Magic Comic** (1939) were to seize a fat slice of the market from the start. Innovations in colour printing, experiments with adventure strips, the creative work of Wilson for A.P. and Watkins for D.C. Thomson of Dundee, all this does indeed make the thirties a period of richness and variety in the history of comics.

What may have been the Golden Age in comics was the 'devil's decade' for ordinary people in Britain, and the tensions and anxieties of the times are reflected in the distorting mirror of the comics. While much of the humour took the form of escapist, wish-fulfilment fantasies in all kinds of contexts, it is equally the case that

[1]Denis Gifford, **Happy Days! A Century of Comics,** London, 1975.
[2]Four of these comics have been reprinted in Denis Gifford's **Penny Comics of the Thirties,** 1975.

L

contemporary fears found embodiment in the figures and situations depicted. Beggars and crooks roam the streets in gangs; the homeless are booted out of doss-houses; shopkeepers palm off shoddy goods on the poor; a fight breaks out between rival candidates for a badly paid job which none of them gets in the end; tramps cheat each other of their last fag-end. Luke and Len the Odd Job Men, whose motto runs 'Willing to Work (If We've Got To)', spend their time in an endless quest for soft jobs, and the jobs and rewards they do get are generally obtained at the expense of others. The 'merry adventures' of Dad Walker and his son Wally in the same comic, **Larks**, originally take them round the world, but in 1936 they are back in London, down on their luck, and their adventures now revolve around ways and means, ingenious or fortuitious, of getting hold of a ten-bob note or a double soss and mash. Thus were the anxieties of the people presented and defused in the penny comics of the twenties and thirties.

Butterfly, Jolly Fun & Sunshine Comic. London: Amalgamated Press. Ed. by Fred Cordwell.
1st series as **Butterfly;** 656 issues; 17 September 1904 to 31 March 1917.
2nd series as **Butterfly and Firefly;** 446 issues; 7 April 1917 to 17 October 1925.
3rd series as **Butterfly;** 760 issues; 24 October 1925 to 18 May 1940.

Comic Cuts, see under section J.

The Favourite Comic, see under section J.

Funny Wonder, see under section J.

Illustrated Chips, see under section J.

The Jester, The Ideal Serio-Comic Journal for Home and "Somewhere." London: Hamsworth Brothers/Amalgamated Press. Ed. by Stanley Gooch.
1st series as **The Wonder and Jester;** 2 issues; 10 and 17 May 1902.
2nd series as **The Jester and Wonder;** 506 issues; 24 May 1902 to 20 January 1912.

3rd series as **The Jester;** 465 issues; 27 January 1912 to 18 December 1920.
4th series as **The Jolly Jester;** 165 issues; 25 December 1920 to 16 February 1924.
5th series as **The Jester;** 847 issues; 23 February 1924 to 18 May 1940.

The Joker. London: Fleetway Press/Amalgamated Press. Ed. by Harold Mansfield (Fleetway)/Richard Chance (A.P.). 655 issues. 5 November 1927 to 18 May 1940.

The Jolly Comic. London: Amalgamated Press. Ed. by Richard Chance. 250 issues. 19 January 1935 to 28 October 1939.

Larks. London: Amalgamated Press. Ed. by Stanley Gooch. 656 issues. 29 October 1927 to 18 May 1940.

Merry and Bright. London: Amalgamated Press. Ed. by Fred Cordwell.
1st series: 337 issues; 22 October 1910 to 31 March 1917.
2nd series: 928 issues; 7 April 1917 to 19 January 1935.

Larks, a typical penny comic of the thirties, was printed on
pink paper. The above issue, no. 471, is dated
31 October 1936.

THE ADVENTURE STRIP

The adventure strip in English comics was a late starter. Excluding the picture stories which had appeared in comics for small children, the first real dramatic strip appeared in **Puck** in 1920, although humorous strips had been known since the 1890s, and despite the strong illustrative tradition of the story-papers. When it did quietly arrive, the 'pictorial story,'[1] as it was sometimes called, was allocated space on the back page only, and remained there for years in such comics as **Merry and Bright, Chips, Jester, Joker** and **Butterfly.** In technique these early attempts at presenting a narrative in a sequence of pictures were far inferior to the humorous strips in the same comics. The characterization was weak (the faces were all the same), and in presentation of action and tension the style of the strips fell far below the illustrations accompanying the serials. Nor was the speech balloon an element which was easily integrated into the narrative strip; it was often filled with inconsequential remarks which diluted the dramatic nature of the text.

The editor did not have far to look for suitable themes; all he needed to do was flick through back numbers of his own comic to find a reservoir of themes, plots, brave young heroes, evil criminals and scheming foreigners. In 1937, for instance, **Comic Cuts** had four dramatic strips running, all thematically related to the serialized stories in the same comic: two detective stories, **Double Crossed** and **The Phantom**; the western **Outlaw's Gold**; and the 'yellow peril' strip **The Trail of Fu Chong**.

The themes may have been easy to adapt, but the art-work and the layout remained unsatisfactory for years. The old story-papers had printed one illustration with each instalment of the serials, illustrations highlighting or foreshadowing crucial scenes in the text. The next step was a number of quite separate pictures (four, five or six) set in long texts, followed by a series of symmetrical pictures (six or nine) with long captions. As late as the 1930s such texts could be as long as 1,500 to 2,000 words in **Merry and Bright** and **Film Fun**; in the latter comic the pictures were initially film stills, then line illustrations in the style of film stills. Adventure films from Hollywood prodded artists into trying out new techniques, not all of which were immediately transferrable to the comic medium: facial close-ups; the fixed camera perspective; the presentation of sweeping movement (the horse thundering across the prairie or the plane zooming across the sky). The wordy captions themselves only began to shrink when speech balloons were used not decoratively, but to express the essence of dialogue, and when the panels were tightened into a sequence which could be easily followed without text. A comic is not 'read' the way a page of print is read; whether by natural reaction or habit, the reader usually scans the pictures first, taking in the gist of the story quickly.

Not that this transition from illustrated text to dramatic strip ran smoothly; early adventure strip artists seem to have made heavy weather of linking panels,

[1]Early terms for the adventure strip or dramatic strip included 'picture-serial', 'picture-thriller', 'pictorial story' and 'story in pictures'.

breaking scenes of action into their smallest constituent parts, in fact, of presenting movement and action of any kind. (A struggle in **Danger Range** in the comic **Butterfly** in 1936 looks more like a stiffly executed dance than a fight-to-the-death.) By the late 1930s, the accompanying text was down to something like 500 to 600 words, but was at the same time an unnecessary appendage to the strip, with interchanges in the speech balloons simply repeated in the small print. When the caption had finally become superfluous, except where a hiatus had to be bridged, or a change in time and place briefly explained, or as in the last frame, where it had an anticipatory function, the entire text in a full-page adventure strip settled down to 200 to 250 words.

Although the adventure strip in its modern form was established in the late thirties, the first real adventure strip in an English comic had actually appeared on 15 May 1920. Drawn by Walter Booth, **Rob the Rover** was serialized in **Puck** for twenty years. By the mid-thirties **Puck** had five adventure strips on four and a half pages, more than any other comic; its closest rival in this respect, **My Favourite**, had four strips on two and a half pages. Both Walter Booth and Arthur Mansbridge adhered to a symmetrical layout of the page, with 5 rows of 3 panels, each panel having a caption of some 50 words. The cramped, static effect of the 15-panel strip was done away with by the young Reg Perrott, whose **Golden Arrow** appeared in **Puck** in 1937. Perrott evidently enjoyed experimenting with sudden switches in perspective, and Tex Ranger, Johnny and Silver Moon frequently find themselves slithering down ravines as rotten rope bridges give under their weight, diving off cliffs into the rapids in order to evade hostile Indians, and falling into geysers only to be spewed out again. Perrott rarely had more than 10 panels to the page, panels he varied in shape and size. He also introduced hand-lettering in captions, generally placed between panels, and speech balloons. Alan Gelli borrowed the technique of hand-lettering, occasionally producing captions in white on black, and added further variety by drawing round-bordered panels.

Adventure strips never looked sturdy enough to dominate a comic, although **Tip Top** and **Jingles** for a time promoted them to page one, only to demote them again later. After the War, the Thomson comics reverted to the old picture-story style in their narrative strips, bringing back long captions and eschewing speech balloons. They did, however, add the element of full colour to Dudley Watkins's back-page retelling of children's classics in **Topper**, beginning with **Treasure Island** in 1953. It was **Eagle** (1950) and **Lion** (1952) and other boys' comics which firmly put an expertly drawn and colour-printed adventure strip on the first three pages, but it had taken over thirty years to get there.

Butterfly, see under section L.

Film Fun. London: Amalgamated Press. Ed. by Fred Cordwell/Philip Davies/Jack LeGrand. 2,225 issues. 17 January 1920 to 8 September 1962. Pre-war circulation 800,000 copies at peak.

Jester, see under section L.

Joker, see under section M.

Larks, see under section L.

My Favourite, see under section K.

Puck, see under section J.

Note the switches in perspective in this adventure strip by Reg Perrott.

EAGLE AND AFTER

Shoe Lane, off Fleet Street, had been the breeding ground for many penny shockers in the late nineteenth century; some six decades later one of the cleanest and brightest and most successful comics ever published for boys was to emerge from the same side street: **Eagle**, conceived and edited by Marcus Morris. A Lancashire vicar and father of four young children, Morris examined the horror comics imported from the States after the war and found them to be 'deplorable, nastily over-violent and obscene'.[1] Many parents agreed but there was a widespread belief at this time that it was the medium, the comic, which was the root cause of the evil; the horror comic was just one ugly head on the hydra. Morris himself, however, was convinced that the adventure strip, which quite evidently fascinated children, could be used 'to convey to the child the right kind of standards, values and attitudes, combined with the necessary amount of excitement and adventure'. The values Morris wished to pass on – decency, courage, fair play, selflessness – were to be embodied in the exemplary character of one Lex Christian who progressed on the drawing-board from being a hard-hitting parson in an East End slum, then a flying padre of the Fighting Seventh, to finally take the form of Dan Dare, Pilot of the Future. **Eagle**, 'Britain's national strip cartoon weekly', published by Hulton Press of Shoe Lane, finally appeared on 14 April 1950.

If the first of the Dan Dare strips appeared stiff and conventional, Frank Hampson, who devised and drew the strip, quickly evolved a style which anticipated later developments in SF strips and films in its creative use of colour and experimental perspective and in its imaginative but precise technology. By scrapping lengthy captions and concentrating the dramatic picture sequences, Hampson brought the adventure strip bang up-to-date. Colonel Dan Dare himself, however, is something of a museum-piece among all this thrilling technology and innovative colour graphics, a throwback to the clean-limbed, righteous Victorian hero. His enemy is his very antithesis, evil, cunning Mekon, *Führer* of a race of green-skinned automatons, the Treens, who arouse fighting instincts in our hero: 'I'm just aching to take a poke at one of those green faces'. In the long run, the 'glorious uppercut' is more than a match for the Treens' sophisticated weaponry. But Dan Dare was not the only hero whose exploits were depicted in the pages of **Eagle**. There were those other defenders of justice, P.C.49, Jeff Arnold, Storm Nelson, and Sergeant 'Tough' Luck. Potted biographies of great men were presented in picture-form on the back pages: Churchill, General Gordon, Baden-Powell, and, in a strip under the title **The Road of Courage**, the life of Jesus.

But **Eagle** was more than the sum of its parts; it had its own very special character, its own integrity. Not only did the editor ensure that his 'strip cartoon paper' was imbued with an unmistakeable moral quality, he also subjected the

---

[1]Marcus Morris, ed., **The Best of 'Eagle'**, London, 1977. The importation of horror comics was – and still is – prohibited under the Children and Young Persons (Harmful Publications) Act, 1955.

language, the printing, the artwork, and the layout to his eagle-eyed scrutiny. His efforts paid off and **Eagle** was an immediate success, eagerly read by children, welcomed by their parents, and warmly reviewed in **The Times Literary Supplement**[2] In 1952 Amalgamated Press brought out their answer to Morris's comic; **Lion** carried a front-page Captain Condor strip by Frank Pepper. **Lion** eventually absorbed **Eagle** in 1969, but Dan Dare was too good a man to keep down and in 1977 he emerged from the deep-freeze to feature in a strip in the most popular of today's adventure comics, **2000 AD**. Perhaps it was just a question of time. In the spring of 1982 **Eagle** was revived as a glossy comic, with most of the adventure stories presented in photo-strip form. But there, in a colour strip drawn by Gerry Embleton to text provided by B.J. Tomlinson, Dan Dare the cosmic knight-errant is back to confront – and, without doubt, finally vanquish – Mekon, the embodiment of all that is evil in this world and the worlds beyond.

Eagle. London: Hulton Press/Longacre Press/Odhams Press/IPC Magazines. Ed. by Rev. Marcus Morris/Clifford Makins. 991 issues. 14 April 1950 to 26 April 1969. Initial circulation approx. 1 million copies.

Eagle (new series). London: IPC Magazines. Ed. by David Hunt. Commenced 27 March 1982 and still being issued. Initial print 350,000 copies; now approx. 150,000 copies p.w.

Eagle Annual. London: Hulton Press/Longacre Press/ Odhams Press/IPC Magazines. 23 annuals appeared between 1952 and 1974; a new series started in 1983.

Lion. London: Amalgamated Press/Fleetway Publications/ IPC Magazines. Ed. by Reginald Eves. Approx. 1,150 issues. 23 February 1952 to 18 May 1974.

2000 AD. London: IPC Magazines. Ed. by 'Tharg'. Commenced 26 February 1977 (earth-time) and still being issued. 150-170,000 copies p.w.

[2]**The Times Literary Supplement** of 6 June 1950.

An early Dan Dare strip by Frank Hampson, from **Eagle** dated 12 June 1953.

TODAY'S PRE-SCHOOL COMICS

Little of the exuberance and charm of the comics produced for young children in the twenties and thirties has washed off onto the comics published for the same age group today. Post-war nursery comics have tended to become a derivative comic form, borrowing their characters and story-lines from other media and sources. Since the sixties, most of them have leaned heavily on children's television programmes instead of inventing ideas and developing characters of their own. In the long-extinct comics **Robin** and **Swift** we had strips about Dixon of Dock Green, Andy Pandy, and Bill and Ben the Flower-Pot Men. This orientation towards television is just as strong today; **Playhour**, to take one example, features the Magic Roundabout on its front page. Many of the other figures in these magazines are borrowed from children's classics such as **Alice in Wonderland** and **The Wind in the Willows**, from fairy-stories, the Bible, and the creations of the Walt Disney Studios.

The picture stories in these comics, generally arranged as symmetrical frames with short captions, seldom with speech balloons, present incidents in the lives of frolicking humanized animals, cute animated dolls and unbelievably well-behaved and neatly dressed children. It is a tidy, comfy world where minor crises on the mummy-can't-find-the-tea-cosy level are solved by magic, happy inspiration, or the last-minute intervention of adults. Mother-figures abound, but fathers only put in an appearance in times of danger and excitement. Daddy is a farmer, doctor, pilot, captain of a liner, policeman or film-director; mummy is mummy. Not all of these picture narratives, however, follow this pattern. Harold Hare's cousin Flopsy has a distinctly unladylike passion for mud, 'in fact, the more muddy she gets – the better she likes it!' Harold's dessicated Aunt Hilda insists that he buy Flopsy a young ladies' toy for her birthday, a doll's tea set. The cousins are mollified, but not for long; in the last frame a delighted Flopsy whizzes down a heap of mud on the tea-tray while a beaming Harold makes mud pies in the cups.

The same 'storytime weekly' – it is **Jack and Jill** – has on its front and back pages a Wombles story. The impact of Elisabeth Beresford's Womble stories, the first one appearing in 1968, may have been diluted when the books were modified for the BBC Television series and then chopped into segments for these brief strips, but children are nevertheless being presented with real inventiveness coupled with light satire in the accounts of these creatures' existence on Wimbledon Common.

Meanwhile, somewhere in suburban Nutwood, a little bear in a red sweater, yellow scarf, check trousers, and Depression boots is setting off on yet another adventure, as his smiling mother and pipe-smoking father wave bye-bye at the gate. Rupert, the **Daily Express's** answer to Teddy Tail, who had been appearing in the **Daily Mail** since 1915, first appeared on 8 November 1920 in a story called 'Little

Lost Bear.' Since then, the modest bear has appeared in some 500 books with sales of over 100 million copies in 18 countries; he has starred in his own ITV show and numerous plays (not forgetting the cartoon film Paul McCartney is working on); he has promoted more than 50 products ranging from umbrellas to toothbrushes; and his own **Rupert Weekly** commenced in the autumn of 1982!

It was Mary Tourtel who created the familiar figure of Rupert and wrote the rhyming couplets which were to become characteristic of the picture stories. In 1935 her premature retirement was brought about by an eye ailment, and her place at the drawing board was taken over by Albert Bestall who himself retired in 1965, although he continued to draw for the annuals. The pre-1935 Rupert lived in a sombre world where evil forces in the shape of ogres and witches constantly threatened to seize power. Bestall, however, changed Rupert from a frightened little bear into an adventure-loving and assertive boy-bear whose world became a greener and happier place. After years at the hands of the artists Alex Cubie and John Harrold, Rupert is today groomed by a team of artists before his daily appearance in just two frames in the **Express**.

Rupert's world is unchanging, timeless, and peaceful. His parents, affectionate and tolerant, never murmur the slightest word of protest as he disappears yet again to unravel some new mystery which has come to his notice; they know their son is neither hothead nor runaway, he will return safely to tell them all about his adventures. The natural leader of his friends Algy (the pup), Bill (the badger), Edward (the elephant), Podgy (the pig) and Pong-Ping (the pekinese), Rupert is also worshipped by those animals who have really remained animals in this symbiotic world. His naive friendliness, helpfulness and generosity are doubtless traits of character which appeal to the old and the young in his band of faithful followers. His innocence and harmonious relationship to nature appealed to the hippies of the late sixties, who made him into something of a cult-figure; for collectors who pay high prices for the old annuals, Rupert provides a nostalgic link with their own youth; parents appreciate the fact that Rupert's family life is happy and reassuring, upholding old-fashioned values of domestic order; children adore the lovable, cheerful bear and enjoy that skilfully controlled and carefully dosed tension in the stories. At 63 years of age, Rupert is as young and wide-eyed and popular as ever.

[1]See W.O.G. Lofts & D.J. Adley, **The Rupert Index: A Bibliography of Rupert Bear**, privately printed, 1979.

Jack and Jill, A Storytime Weekly. London: Amalgamated Press/Fleetway Publications/IPC Magazines. Ed. by Stewart Pride. First issue dated 27 February 1954; still running.

Playhour, A Storytime Weekly. London: Amalgamated Press/Fleetway Publications/IPC Magazines. Ed. by Stewart Pride. First issue 21 May 1955 and still appearing.

Robin. London: Hulton Press/Longacre Press/Odhams Press/IPC Magazines. Ed. by Rev. Marcus Morris. 836 issues. 28 March 1953 to 25 January 1969.

Rupert (Adventure Series). London: Daily Express. 50 issues. September 1948 to June 1963.

Rupert. London: Jeenaroy Ltd. 4 nos. 1976-77.

Rupert Weekly. London: Marvel Comics Ltd. Commenced 20 October 1982 and still being issued.

Rupert Annual. London: Daily Express. 47 annuals have appeared since the first one was issued in 1936 (dated 1937).
Lofts & Adley have estimated total sales to 1978 at 34 million copies.

Swift. London: Hulton Press/Longacre Press. Ed. by Rev. Marcus Morris/Clifford Makins. 477 issues. 20 March 1954 to 2 March 1963.

Twinkle, Specially for Little Girls. London: D. C. Thomson. Commenced on 27 January 1968 and still being issued.

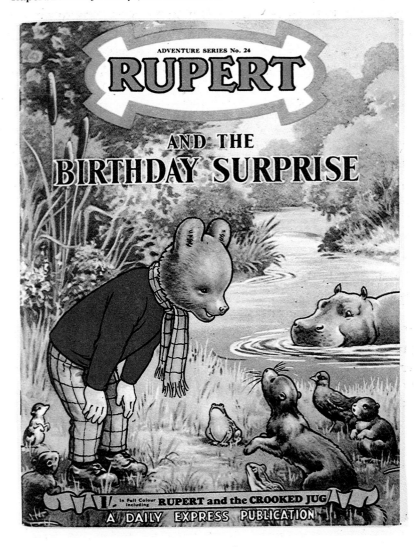

Devotees will want to count the horizontal bands on Rupert's trousers (there should be six).

DANDY, BEANO AND CLAN

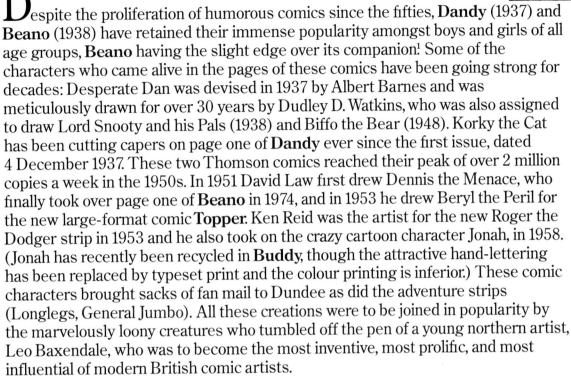

Despite the proliferation of humorous comics since the fifties, **Dandy** (1937) and **Beano** (1938) have retained their immense popularity amongst boys and girls of all age groups, **Beano** having the slight edge over its companion! Some of the characters who came alive in the pages of these comics have been going strong for decades: Desperate Dan was devised in 1937 by Albert Barnes and was meticulously drawn for over 30 years by Dudley D. Watkins, who was also assigned to draw Lord Snooty and his Pals (1938) and Biffo the Bear (1948). Korky the Cat has been cutting capers on page one of **Dandy** ever since the first issue, dated 4 December 1937. These two Thomson comics reached their peak of over 2 million copies a week in the 1950s. In 1951 David Law first drew Dennis the Menace, who finally took over page one of **Beano** in 1974, and in 1953 he drew Beryl the Peril for the new large-format comic **Topper**. Ken Reid was the artist for the new Roger the Dodger strip in 1953 and he also took on the crazy cartoon character Jonah, in 1958. (Jonah has recently been recycled in **Buddy**, though the attractive hand-lettering has been replaced by typeset print and the colour printing is inferior.) These comic characters brought sacks of fan mail to Dundee as did the adventure strips (Longlegs, General Jumbo). All these creations were to be joined in popularity by the marvelously loony creatures who tumbled off the pen of a young northern artist, Leo Baxendale, who was to become the most inventive, most prolific, and most influential of modern British comic artists.

Baxendale's first successful cartoon in **Beano** was a Red Indian Dennis the Menace by the name of Little Plum your Redskin Chum (1953), followed in the same year by a female Dennis the Menace named Minnie the Minx, a boisterous, shamelessly egotistic girl who specialised in pulverising boys, singly or in gangs. Anarchy exploded in **When the Bell Rings** (1954) which depicted the uproar that took place when school was over, in a large panel in the Casey Court tradition. This series developed into a full-page cartoon under a new title, The Bash Street Kids, in 1956, the year in which Baxendale started work on The Banana Bunch for the **Beezer**. A few years later the Three Bears parted company with Little Plum to do their own thing in a **Beano** strip (1959). Baxendale left Thomson's in 1964 to devise the comic **Wham!** for Odhams Press, producing a new range of odd characters, among them Eagle-Eye the Junior Spy, Grimly Feendish, and General Nutt and his Barmy Army, while Ken Reid obviously thoroughly enjoyed drawing Frankie Stein and Jasper the Grasper. **Wham!** appeared at a time when the comics market was dwindling; at twice the price of the Thomson comics, and with a penchant for parody that must have appealed to a slightly older age group, it never really got off the ground. From 1966 to 1975 Baxendale worked for IPC Magazines, continuing to do undercover work for Odhams from Kingleo Studios. By the early seventies he

P

[1] The findings of the Schools Council report **Children and Their Books**, 1977, were confirmed in **Language Performance in Schools**, HMSO, 1983.

had worked for virtually all post-war humorous comics,[2] and had seen his style adopted and adapted by many other artists. The features he drew in the 1950s still appear in **Beano**. In 1975 Baxendale left British comics, hatching new plans for work since issued by Duckworth in the U.K. and publishers in Belgium and Holland.[3]

There are probably few children in Britain today, and few parents, who are not familiar with the world of **Dandy** and **Beano**. The rituals, the tom-foolery, the table-turning, the awful puns have changed little over the years. It is a never-never-land where the upper and lower classes get on famously (Lord Snooty); where mortar-boarded teachers are bound and gagged as the whole class plays truant to watch the local football derby (Bash Street Kids); where a sneeze can bend lampposts and send cars flying over rooftops (Desperate Dan); where the cupidity of bears surpasses that of humans; where violence produces feelings of fury or humiliation, but rarely pain (despite the gigantic lumps and miles of bandages). Rebellious youth fearlessly challenges authority in these comics, and the impulse to lawlessness and disorder is on balance only just contained by Law and Order in various guises. Impossible parents, teachers and policemen may sometimes be put in their places, humiliated or out-manoeuvred, but more often revolt is quelled by the traditional 'whacking'. Aggressiveness, egoism, greed, dreams about being super-strong, 'these recurrent themes echo children's moods and fantasies', Nicholas Tucker has written, adding that violence in society and in personality is acknowledged in these comics, but neutralized by humour.[4] Perhaps it is just this working-out of dreams and conflicts in the zany world of **Dandy** and **Beano** that accounts for their long-running success. At any rate, it is a frequently observed phenomenon that children study and savour their favourite characters, and take their funny comics very seriously indeed.

[2]He worked for **Beano** (1953-62), **Wizard** (1955), **Beezer** (1956-64), **Wham!** (1964-66), **Smash!** (1966-69), **Buster** (1966-68, 1970-75), **Valiant** (1966-70), **Lion** (1968), **Jag** (1968), **Whizzer and Chips** (1969), **Jet** (1971), **Knockout** (1971), **Shiver and Shake** (1973), **Monster Fun** (1975).
[3]See Baxendale's own account of his time in the comics industry, **A Very Funny Business**, London, 1978.
[4]Nicholas Tucker, 'Comics Today,' in his **Suitable for Children?**, London, 1976.

The Beano (originally **The Beano Comic**). London: D. C. Thomson. Ed. by George Moonie/Harold Cramond. Commenced 30 July 1938 and still being issued. Peak circulation reputedly around 2 million copies p.w.

The Beezer. London: D. C. Thomson. Ed. by Iain Chisholm/Bill Swinton. Commenced 21 January 1956 and still running.

Buddy, All That's Best For Boys. London: D. C. Thomson. First issue dated 14 February 1981.

Cor!! London: IPC Magazines. Ed. by Bob Paynter. 210 issues. 6 June 1970 to 15 June 1974.

The Dandy (originally **The Dandy Comic**). London: D. C. Thomson. Ed. to April 1982 by Albert Barnes, now by David Torrie. Commenced 4 December 1937 and still being issued. Circulation reputedly around 2 million in the fifties.

Knockout. London: Amalgamated Press/Fleetway Publications. Ed. by Montagu Haydon/H. O'Mant/Leonard Matthews. 1,251 issues. 4 March 1939 to 16 February 1963.

Pow! London: Odhams Press. Ed. by Alf Wallace. 86 issues. 21 January 1967 to 7 September 1968.

Pow!, Smash! and **Wham!** (see below) also featured Marvel's superheroes.

Radio Fun. London: Amalgamated Press. Ed. by Stanley Gooch. 1,167 issues. 15 October 1938 to 18 February 1961.

Shiver and Shake. London: IPC Magazines. Ed. by Bob Paynter. 83 issues. 10 March 1973 to 5 October 1974.

Smash! London: Odhams Press/IPC Magazines. Ed. by Alf Wallace. 265 issues. 5 February 1966 to 3 April 1971.

The Topper. London: D. C. Thomson. Ed. by Ron Fraser. Commenced 7 February 1953 and still appearing.

T.V. Fun. London: Amalgamated Press. Ed. by Stanley Gooch. 312 issues. 19 September 1953 to 5 September 1959.

Wham! London: Odhams Press. Ed. by Alf Wallace. 187 issues. 20 June 1964 to 13 January 1968.

Whizzer and Chips. London: IPC Magazines. Ed. by Bob Paynter. Commenced 18 October 1969 and is still being issued.

© D.C.Thomson and Co.Ltd.1961

Leo Baxendale's Minnie the Minx seldom took 'no' for an answer, especially from boys. 3 panels from a 15-panel strip in **The Beano** dated 13 May 1961.

The Dandy, one of the most popular humorous comics
in Britain today, first appeared in 1937. The other is its
sister The Beano, which first appeared in 1938.

Dennis the Menace drawn by David Law from **The Beano**
dated 15 October 1960.

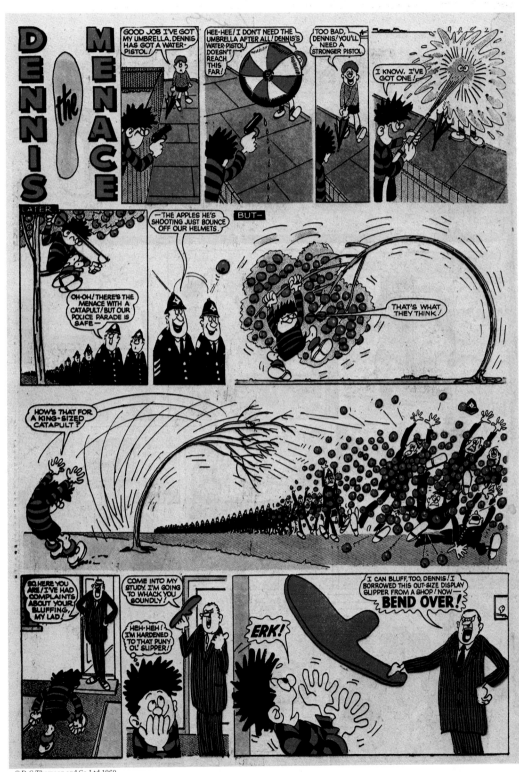

Beryl the Peril, drawn by David Law, first appeared in
The Topper in 1953. The issue reprinted above is dated
31 August 1957.

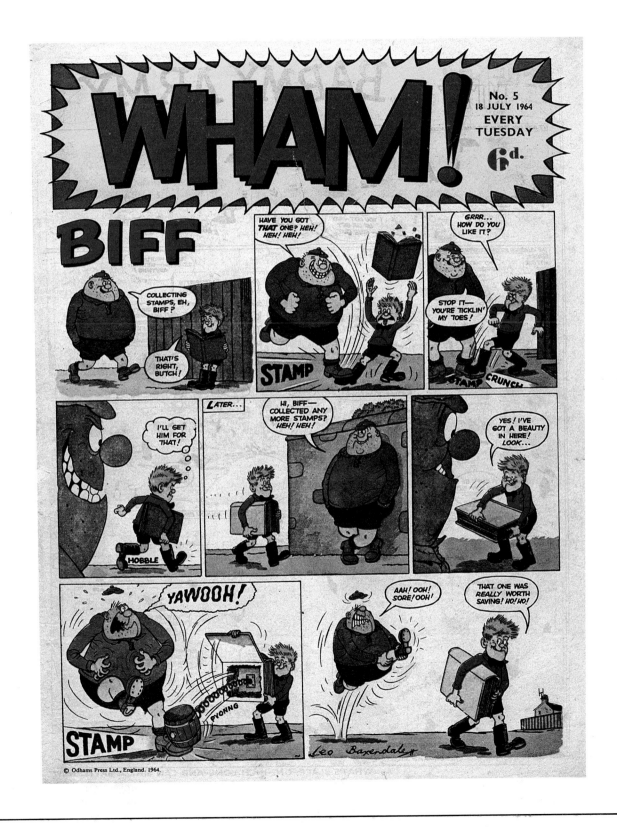

Jonah, originally drawn by Ken Reid for **The Beano,** now appears in the comic **Buddy.**

The Bash Street Kids, drawn by Leo Baxendale, originally appeared in **The Beano** in a strip called **When the Bell Rings.**

'Desperate Dan, the cowboy of massive, bristled chin, superhuman strength and kindly, gullible nature [...] is always at his happiest seated at a table in front of his daily diet of Cow Pie, a species of that dish which comprehends the whole of the animal, including horns and tail which project through the pastry.' **(The Times)**

Keyhole Kate, drawn by Allan Morley, was based on the strips 'Paul & Pearl Pryor' by Roy Wilson in **Larks** and 'Selena Pry' by George Wakefield in **Butterfly.**

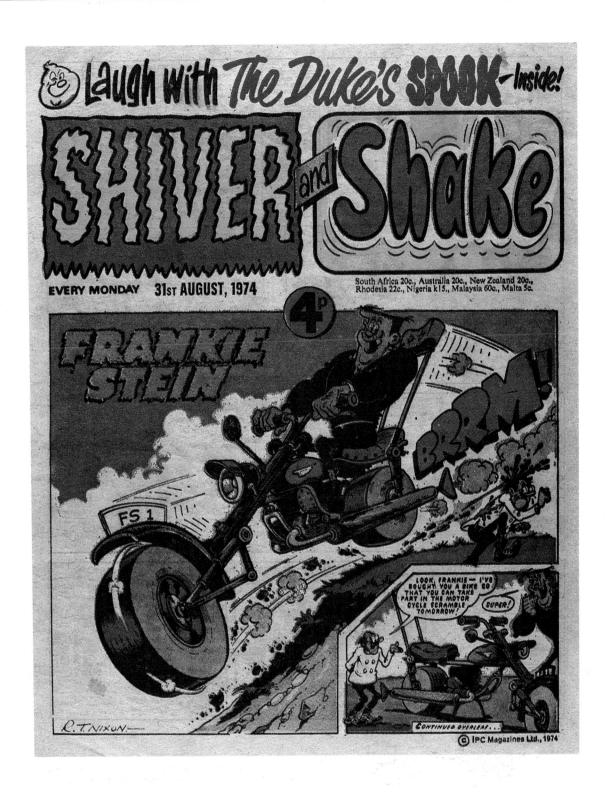

GIRLS' COMICS

The **School Friend,** the first girls' comic published in Britain after the war, appeared in May 1950 and was soon selling a million copies a week. **Girl** followed in early 1951 and in March 1953 the popular story-paper **Girls' Crystal** was transformed overnight into a picture-paper. The subjects of the picture serials were traditional: school and sport; horses; mystery and adventure; the privations of jungle girls and Crusoe girls. At this time – the early fifties – teenage girls in working-class families were being thrilled by the 'sensational romances' and 'pulsating love dramas' printed in periodicals such as **The Miracle** and **The Oracle**, which contained one romantic story in picture-strip form in every issue. These periodicals were themselves replaced in the late fifties by the 'great all-picture love story weeklies' **Marilyn** (the first comic consisting of romantic picture stories), **Romeo, Valentine** and others. By the mid-sixties these comics still had a fifties flavour about them, they were too sloppy and too predictable, and one by one they expired leaving the field to an extraordinarily popular girls' magazine, **Jackie,** a magazine which was responsive both to its readers' interests and to the boom in the entertainment and luxury articles industry. Since the 1960s, the increasing diversification of the comic market by age as well as sex has split the girls' comic sector into three main groups: magazines for learning readers (**Twinkle,** for 3 to 7 years); picture-story papers for the age group 8 to 11 years (**Bunty, Judy, Mandy, Tammy** and many others); and the magazines for the 11 to 15 year age bracket (**Jackie** and others).

The **Bunty** group of comics are all basically similar in graphics and content; their picture-stories are conventional in technique, although one of them, **Debbie,** has photo-stories (a feature of magazines for older girls). The fiction in these comics contains strong elements of mystery and the occult. A single recent issue of **Bunty** has tales about an extra-terrestrial being which has adopted the form of a girl to explore life on this planet; a hypnotic and apparently indestructible doll that recharges itself on the energy released in the aggression it produces in human beings; a universe behind the Spectrum Door where time dashes madly – backwards; a gipsy who casts a spell on a promising young ballerina; a young girl who finds an old magic book. Far more striking, however, is the predominance of a particular kind of main character in the serials, a girl who turns out to be sick, misunderstood, or persecuted. There are orphans sadistically maltreated by their grasping guardians; girls forced into a life of crime by Fagin-like old hags; girls wrongly accused of theft; youngsters suffering from amnesia and taken in by unscrupulous roving junk dealers; lonely ballerinas who are prevented from developing their talents by spiteful stepmothers; wheelchair girls who yearn to become athletes; pale, fragile girls with terminal illnesses. Many of these girls devise ways and means of defeating the hostile adults who are ruining their lives.

[1] L. Fenwick, 'Periodicals and Adolescent Girls', in **Studies in Education**, vol. 2, no. 1, 1953.

But some, blaming themselves for being spurned, or positively enjoying their handicap for the sympathy elicited from others. The 'suffering angel' is a persistent feature of these comics, although the IPC products all in all tend to be more lively, adventure-oriented, and down-to-earth than the Thomson group. If the hoydenish heroine or 'little wildcat' of the earlier story-papers is to be found anywhere, it will be in IPC's **Tammy** or **Jinty**.

One of the findings of the Schools Council report on children's reading, published in 1977, was that at all age-levels girls read considerably more periodicals than boys. In recent years, publishers have turned their attention to the sector of the market which had previously been dominated by one magazine, **Jackie**. Whereas **Jackie** was cautious and above all decent about sexual matters, the new generation of girls' glossy magazines appearing since the late seventies – among them **Oh Boy!**, **My Guy**, **Mates**, **Love Affair** – do not beat about the bush when it comes to sex: it is clearly their main focus of interest. In a recent story, Sharon, determined to punish her fella Jeff for not devoting enough time to her (he is revising for exams), makes a rendezvous in the garden shed with Dave, another boy from her class. She is not disappointed with her choice: 'He was far more physical than Jeff – and so randy!' Sex, fashion and pop are among the interests these magazines cater for, and the consumer mentality which is being encouraged is underlined by the volume of advertising and related material included (around 6 to 8 – in one case 14 or 15 – pages out of 32). What is really shocking about these magazines is the correspondence page, consisting of letters which testify to the profound unhappiness and confusion of young teenage girls.

The replies, to be fair, are on the whole both sympathetic and level-headed, and there is some weight to the argument that these magazines are catering for a need which is not met elsewhere, at home or school. Parents may have their doubts about the grab-a-guy morality of the **Oh Boy!** class of weeklies, but there can be no doubt about their popularity, with their total audited circulation of some 2 million copies per week, each copy reaching an estimated four readers.[2]

[2]Figures from Barbara Griggs, 'Today's Thrills', in **The Sunday Times**, 28 June 1981.

Boyfriend. London: City Magazines. Ed. R. Taylor. 428 issues. 16 May 1959 to 2 September 1967.

Bunty. London: D. C. Thomson. First issue dated 18 January 1958; still appearing.

Cherie, Exciting Love Stories in Pictures. London: D. C. Thomson. 160 issues. 1 October 1960 to 19 October 1963.

Debbie. London: D. C. Thomson. First issue dated 17 February 1973; discontinued.

Girl, Sister Paper to **Eagle.** London: Hulton Press/Longacre Press/IPC Magazines. 664 issues. 2 November 1951 to 3 October 1964.

Girl, Your Very Best Friend. London: IPC Magazines. Ed. by Evelyn Cohen. Commenced February 1981 and still being issued.

Jackie, For Go-Ahead Teens. London: D. C. Thomson. First issue dated 11 January 1964; still running.

Jinty. London: IPC Magazines. First issue dated 11 May 1974 and still appearing.

Judy. London: D. C. Thomson. Commenced 16 January 1960 and is still being issued.

Mandy. London: D. C. Thomson. Commenced 21 January 1967 and is still being issued.

Marilyn, The Great All-Picture Love Story Weekly. London: Amalgamated Press/Fleetway Publications. Ed. by R. A. Lewis. 547 issues. 19 March 1955 to 18 September 1965.

Marty, First Ever Photo Romance Weekly/Romantic All-Picture Love Stories. London: C. Arthur Pearson. 162 issues. 23 January 1960 to 23 February 1963.

Mirabelle. London: C. Arthur Pearson/IPC Magazines. 1,009 issues. 10 September 1956 to 22 October 1977.

Romeo. London: D. C. Thomson. Approx. 885 issues. 31 August 1957 to 14 September 1974.

Roxy. London: Amalgamated Press/Fleetway Publications. Approx. 285 issues (not numbered). 15 March 1958 to 14 September 1963.

School Friend, The Only Schoolgirls' Paper in the World. London: Amalgamated Press. 766 issues. 20 May 1950 to 23 January 1965.
Initial circulation around 1 million copies p.w.

Tammy. London: IPC Magazines. Ed. by G. Finley-Day. Commenced 6 February 1971 and still running.

Tracy, Picture-Stories for Girls. London: D. C. Thomson. Commenced 6 October 1979 and is still being issued.

Valentine, Brings You Love Stories in Pictures. London: Amalgamated Press/Fleetway Publications/IPC Magazines. Ed. by R. A. Lewis. Approx. 720 issues. 19 January 1957 to 9 November 1974.

'The kiss I had been waiting for all my life' traditionally concluded the romantic picture stories in the **Valentine** group of girls' comics.

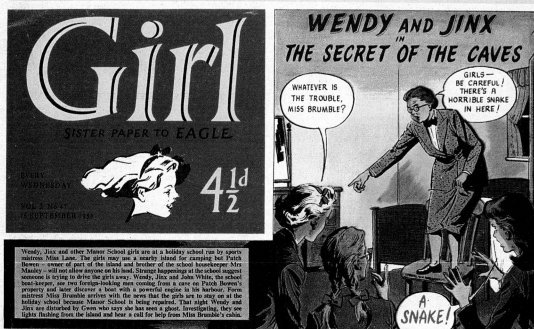

Two of D. C. Thomson's popular girls' comics.

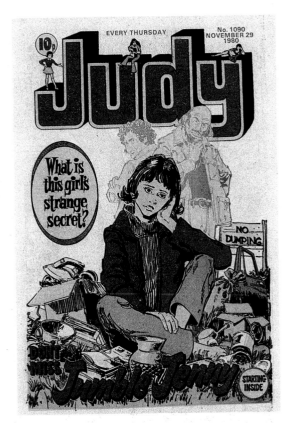

WAR COMICS

'Schweinhund! The Flammenwerfer for you!...Aaaaaargh!'
'Too slow, Kraut!'

The Second World War went on raging, fictionally, in the boys' adventure comics and war comics which D. C. Thomson and IPC Magazines have been producing for over twenty years. Early trends towards war comics can be traced by looking at a few old issues of **Knockout**, a humorous comic in the 1950s but one which began to feature Battler Britain on its first three pages in 1961. In the fifties, the general adventure comic **Lion** had carried a short war strip tucked away on its inside pages, but by 1966 this had become a four-page splash, **Trelawney of the Guards**, five pages including the front-cover illustration. The war 'libraries' still being issued today originally commenced between 1958 and 1961, but these productions seem amateurish and tame in comparison with the new war comics **Warlord** (1974), **Battle** (1975) and **Bullet** (1976), with their contrasting colours, screaming close-ups, and borderless panels which crash into each other as the action races on. Apart from the usual serial strips, these comics contain an astonishing variety of supplementary material on the apparently inexhaustible subject of war: descriptions of weapons systems; photos and cross-sections of tanks, destroyers and jet fighters; reviews of war films; quizzes on battles; anecdotes about famous soldiers; adverts for war toys; recruitment ads; even accounts of RAF-Luftwaffe reunions.

Battle may have recently presented the Falklands campaign in strip-form, but the war which fires the imagination of youth – the publishers claim – is the 1939-45 War, and here boys are in step with their elders, whose obsession with the last world war is fuelled by TV, Hollywood and the paperback industry. Perhaps this widespread passionate interest is just nostalgia for a time of greatness, the memory of an ultimately successful war against dictatorship and oppression, or perhaps it is a form of pining for something politicians constantly seem to be striving to recover, real national unity.

If the bulk of war strips go back to the war against fascism, the SF-cum-war comic **2000 AD** looks to future military struggles, reporting on the attempts by Judge Dredd and fellow Mega City judges to hold up the advance of the East-Meg army; and war-strip addicts will be pleased to note that even after the nuclear holocaust there is still a secluded spot on Nu-Earth where traditional warfare 'in all its many and terrifying guises' can be waged with accustomed fury. **2000AD**, however, does not strictly belong to the war comics, most of which present authentic and fictional accounts of British participation in the last war.

The enemy is almost invariably German or Japanese, presented at best as slow-witted dupes, at worst as beasts who deserve the death meted out to them. The heroes are, as a rule, British soldiers and airmen, powerfully built, tough warriors whose will to fight will only be increased by peril, torture or incarceration.

A long-standing sub-theme in the war comic (but one which has receded in recent years with the coming of the ruthless killer as hero) concerns the fighting man with a character defect which is eradicated by war, or the soldier who because of negligent upbringing thinks little of fighting, until he sees action; or the soldier who regards himself as a coward but whose real bravery emerges when the going gets tough. War cleanses the blood. Some would say that what these comics present is effectively a glorification of war, a picture of manliness and individual heroism which may seem absurd or irrelevant in an age of computer-guided Exocet missiles and thermo-nuclear bombs. The horrific biological and psychological reality of war, or the conflicts leading to wars are not acknowledged, and perhaps could not easily be acknowledged in the comic paper format.

The child who reads several of these comics a week is imbibing a strong brew. Although it was convincingly demonstrated some years ago that war comic readers are likely to have a stereotyped picture of foreigners,[1] the answers to questions about the effects of this reading matter and the reasons why war fiction is such compelling reading for the young remain speculative. John Heeley has recently suggested that the merciless brutality and inhumanity of the war comics 'meet the needs of certain social groups and are a reflection of the patriotic, authoritarian, "dog eats dog" mentality of the British people', and that these comics 'help inculcate a particular definition of violence, one which sees it as normal, natural and inevitable.'[2] His views have been energetically contested, and in any case war comics are not one of the expanding areas of the market. It is clear nonetheless that modern children's periodicals, no less than those of the 1860s, are capable of arousing strong controversy.

---

[1]Nicholas Johnson, 'What Do Children Learn from War Comics?' in **New Society**, 7 July 1966.
[2]John Heeley, 'Boys' Comics: Violence Rules', in **The Sunday Times**, 27 February 1983.

Action. London IPC Magazines.
1st series: 42 issues; 14 February to 27 November 1976.
2nd series: 50 issues; 4 December 1976 to 12 November 1977.
Amalgamated with **Battle** after the W. H. Smith chain refused to handle it on account of the excessive violence of its strips, not all of which were on the theme of war.

Battle. London: IPC Magazines. Commenced on 8 March 1975 and still being issued.
Appeared under the title **Battle Picture Weekly** from 8 March 1975 to 12 November 1977, then **Battle Action,** and is now simply called **Battle.**

Battle Picture Library. London: Fleetway Publications/IPC Magazines. Ed. by Ted Bensberg. Commenced in January 1961 and still running.

Bullet. London: D. C. Thomson. 147 issues. 14 February 1976 to 2 December 1978.

Commando, War Stories in Pictures. London: John Leng & D. C. Thomson/D. C. Thomson. Commenced in July 1961 and is still being issued.

Fury. Sevenoaks, Kent: Marvel Comics. Commenced 16 March 1977 and discontinued the same year.

Knockout, see under section P.

Lion, see under section N.

2000 AD, see under section N.

Valiant. London: IPC Magazines. Ed. by Jack LeGrand. 730 issues. 6 October 1962 to 16 October 1976.
Was selling 500,000 copies p.w. in the early seventies.

Victor. London: D. C. Thomson. Commenced on 25 February 1961 and is still being issued.

Warlord. London: D. C. Thomson. Commenced 28 September 1974 and is still being issued.

War Picture Library. London: Amalgamated Press/Fleetway Publications/IPC Magazines. Ed. Vernon Holding/Ted Bensberg. Commenced in September 1958 and still running.

The return of Neanderthal Man disguised as a Nazi soldier.
Battle Action dated 3 January 1981.

INDEX